# THE BEST BIG IDEAS FOR YOUTH GROUPS

## Patrick A
## and Nick A

## Marshall Pickering
*An Imprint of* HarperCollins*Publishers*

Marshall Pickering is an imprint of
HarperCollins*Religious*
part of HarperCollins*Publishers*
77–85 Fulham Palace Road, London W6 8JB
www.christian-publishing.co.uk

First published in Great Britain in 1999
by Marshall Pickering

1 3 5 7 9 10 8 6 4 2

A catalogue record for this book
is available from the British Library

ISBN 0 551 03240 5

Printed and bound in Great Britain by
Caledonian International Book Manufacturing Ltd, Glasgow

# CONTENTS

# ICE-BREAKERS

# Why Use Ice-Breakers?

It's eight o'clock on Sunday evening. Ten young people have arrived so far. A few of these have drifted in from the Evening Service, others from watching TV, hanging out with friends, playing afternoon sport or doing homework. Some might be feeling nervous or shy about what will happen at the meeting; others may be excited and enthusiastic; for others this might be the highlight of their week – the chance to meet with friends from different schools ...

For us as youth leaders, this makes the way in which we begin the evening really important. Ice-breakers are a great way of getting young people mixing, moving, belonging and participating almost without them realizing it. This part of the book contains a number of our favourite ice-breakers, divided up into four types. We hope that you will have as much fun with them as we do.

## GETTING TO KNOW YOU

These are activities for new groups, or for when new members come along. They are also very useful for challenging cliques and encouraging people to mix more beyond their own friendship circles.

## EVERYBODY INCLUDED

These ice-breakers involve and include everyone, either as teams or as individuals. They often involve movement, they sometimes require food, but they are always lots of fun. They get the group buzzing at the start of the evening or provide a lively insertion between one section and another.

## VOLUNTEERS ONLY

These are up-front activities, and some of them are
disgusting! Only some of your youth group members will be
willing to do things such as sucking baked beans up a
hosepipe, but everyone will love to watch them do it! Some
have the potential to be so embarrassing that a shy person,
if forced to take part, would be put off the group for ever. In
these volunteer-only games it's perfectly OK to offer prizes
(i.e. bribes) and to use peer-group pressure or any appropriate means to persuade your young people to participate,
providing that no one is participating against their will.

## OPENING UP

These ice-breakers connect more to feelings and emotions,
thoughts and expressions. They involve a greater degree of
trust from the young people, and so they must be used with
care. They can create opportunities for young people to
share openly and honestly about themselves.

# Ten Reasons for Using Ice-Breakers

1. Ice-breakers set the tone and feel for the rest of the evening. A good start can make the whole meeting go well; a bad start can result in a lacklustre evening.

2. Ice-breakers define the style of the group, helping the young people develop a group identity.

3. Ice-breakers produce a participative opening experience for newcomers to the group; this can help to make them feel part of the group. It is much easier to belong and then to believe than it is to believe and then to belong.

4. Ice-breakers can build up self-confidence and self-esteem, creating an atmosphere where it is safe to join in and, more importantly, safe not to win. (So we should not let the games become too competitive.)

5. Ice-breakers act as a transition from the rest of the day. At Soulfire (an ecumenical youth worship event), we always start with an up-front, volunteers-only activity. This marks a change from the ordinary activities of the day; it's a move into something different and allows people to adjust.

**6.** Ice-breakers provide shared experiences which can be discussed beyond the group, at school or college etc. – experiences that are safe and fun to share.

**7.** Ice-breakers show that Christians are normal – they are people who can have fun and a laugh. This is important, since one of the problems with evangelism among young people is the preconception that Christians are boring.

**8.** Ice-breakers create a safe opportunity for sharing ideas and thoughts. Many young people today feel that they have very few real friends, and so opportunities to share in this way can be highly treasured.

**9.** Ice-breakers provide a way of connecting to the programme for those kids who find it difficult to sit still for very long and who learn more effectively when they are active.

**10.** Last but not least, ice-breakers at the beginning of an evening create time for late-comers to arrive without disrupting the meeting.

# GETTING TO KNOW YOU

# Colour Clash

## AIM

Ice-breaker, conversation starter, discussion warm-up.

## HOW TO PLAY

1. Get all the group to call out their favourite colour.

2. Everyone has to find a partner with a different colour.

3. Each person has three minutes to persuade their partner that they should change favourite colour to theirs, by any means.

4. After several minutes call a halt (over the row!) and find out how many have changed favourite colours.

## VARIATIONS

1. Use football teams, pop groups etc. as appropriate.

2. Have one pair persuading another pair.

# HINTS

A good game to lead onto something else. For example, split into teams to look at the question: 'Why are so few people persuaded by argument to become Christians, compared with the number of those who are led to Christ by friends or family?'

# Clumping

## AIM

To get the young people into groups of a particular size, and to get them warmed up and moving about.

## EQUIPMENT

A loud voice.

## HOW TO PLAY

The young people have to mingle until a number is yelled out, at which point they have to get into groups of that number and sit down in their group. Those left standing can be eliminated, or lose a chance/life, or do a forfeit. They stand again when the leader yells 'mingle'. Then the leader yells another number and the process continues.

## VARIATIONS

1. Non-competitive, with no forfeits or eliminations.

2. After the number is called everyone has to touch the wall before forming a 'clump'.

3. When formed, 'clumps' have to link arms and face inwards or outwards.

**4.** If using lives, the two who have lost the least number of lives (the winners!) have to make the drinks, tidy the chairs, etc.

# Talk Down

## AIM

To get the young people to consider what a conversation is about (i.e. listening and *not* just talking!).

## HOW TO PLAY

1. Everyone is in pairs.

2. The objective is to hold a conversation, but to talk about what *you* want to talk about, not what your partner wants to talk about.

3. Sit back and let them talk.

## CONCLUSION

You can debrief the game and get people to share how they felt when their partner would not listen. Or move from this activity into another talking ice-breaker.

## HINT

The level of noise will grow progressively louder and louder.

## Silent Organization

## AIM

Mixer, ice-breaker, method of dividing the group into teams.

## HOW TO PLAY

1.  Everyone in the group sits on a chair in a large semi-circle. Ask them to stand on their chairs.

2.  Then ask them to put themselves into order of height, with the tallest at one end of the chairs and the shortest at the other. The only rules are:
    (a) They are not allowed to talk.
    (b) They are not allowed to step on the floor.
    (c) Anyone who breaks either of the above rules has to restart at the end furthest from where they are aiming to get to in the semi-circle.

3.  When they are organized you can then count them off into teams – 1, 2, 3, 4, 1, 2, 3, 4 and so on – so that there is a fair distribution of heights for a subsequent game.

## VARIATIONS

Instead of using height, use age, birthdays, length of time as a Christian, or length of time as a church-goer. Talking may be necessary.

# Week Ending

## AIM

To assist group integration.

## HOW TO PLAY

1.  Ask all the group to pair off with someone they have not spoken to over the past week.

2.  Giving each person two minutes, ask them to take turns in explaining in detail to their partner what they have done over the past week.

3.  When that has been done, ask them to join up with another pair, then each person in turn explains what their partner has been up to over the past seven days.

4.  When everyone has finished, continue with the main activity of the evening.

# Crazy Mixer

## AIM

A start-of-term mixer – a fun activity for when new members join.

## EQUIPMENT

A pencil and a Crazy Mixer Sheet for each person.

## HOW TO PLAY

Move around the room asking people to carry out the various tasks on the sheet. Each time a person performs one of the tasks or allows you to do one of the tasks to them they are to sign next to that action on the sheet. You can only have the same person sign the sheet twice for small groups or once for large groups. The winner is the first person to complete all the tasks.

# Crazy Mixer Sheet

**1.** Get five people to write their names out in full (including any really embarrassing middle names!) on the back of this sheet.

**2.** Unlace somebody's shoe.

**3.** Leapfrog over somebody five times.

**4.** Get a hair from someone's head (let them remove it!).

**5.** Get someone to do a somersault.

**6.** Get someone of the opposite gender to do five press-ups.

**7.** Sing the National Anthem to someone.

**8.** Play 'Ring a ring of roses' with someone (out loud!).

**9.** Find someone who has the same number of letters in their first name as you and arm-wrestle them.

**10.** Change an item of clothing with someone.

# Back to Back

## AIM

Fun.

## HOW TO PLAY

This game is immensely simple and only takes a matter of minutes. Gather people together in pairs. It helps if they are roughly equal in height. Get them to stand back to back. They must then lean against each other and sit down without using their hands! Very simple.

Now they have to stand up again, leaning against each other and not using their arms. Some pairs will achieve this very easily, some will not be so fortunate. But ask them to do it three or four times.

## VARIATIONS

Ask them to join up with another pair and to stand in a square back to back, leaning against each other. Then ask them to sit down and stand up. This variation usually produces a lot of laughs and bodies all over the floor! Ask them to do it a few times.

# HINTS

If they are having real problems, particularly in a group of four, allow them to link their arms together. It actually makes things a lot easier. Take care to exclude sensitively anyone who has a back problem.

## Money Madness

## AIM

A group mixer.

## EQUIPMENT

Each person needs a 'Money Madness Instructions Sheet' and three facsimile £5 notes.

## HOW TO PLAY

1. Everyone has to follow the instructions on the 'Money Madness Instructions Sheet'. The object of the game is to be the one who accumulates the most (or loses the least!) money within a given time period.

2. At intervals throughout the game the leader yells out the word 'Scramble!' or blows a whistle. When he/she does this, all the players must throw £5 into the air. If they get it back, great; if not, someone else gets it!

# Money Madness Instruction Sheet

**1.** Find someone of the same sex. Add up all the letters of your Christian names and your surname. The competitor with the most letters wins £5 from the loser.

**2.** Find someone who wears glasses or contact lenses. Say 'ahhhhh' together until one person runs out of breath. Whoever can say 'ahhhhh' for the longest time wins £5 from the loser.

**3.** If you are down to only £5 you can collect £5 from anyone who has more than three £5 notes. (You can only do this once.)

**4.** Find someone you don't know well. Both of you must sing the National Anthem one word at a time, alternating between the two of you. The first person to make a mistake gives £5 to the other person.

**5.** Find someone who looks younger than you. Play 'paper-scissors-stone'. The first person who wins twice collects £5 from the loser.

**6.** Find someone who is the same height as you. They must swap their money with you.

# EVERYBODY INCLUDED

# Grab

## AIM

Warm-up, ice-breaker.

## EQUIPMENT

One chair per person, a shoe or ball or bone.

## PREPARATION

Lay the chairs out in two lines, facing each other.

## HOW TO PLAY

1. Each person sits on a chair. Number them off, starting from opposite ends of the two lines.

   ```
   1 2 3 4 5 6 7 8
           X
   8 7 6 5 4 3 2 1
   ```

2. The ball or bone is placed in the middle at 'x' and a number is called.

3. Both players with that number try to grab the ball. The one who gets it first tries to return to his or her seat without being tagged by the other.

**4.** If the player gets back untagged the team score a point; if they are tagged, then the other team scores a point.

## HINT

Keep it fast and encourage them to use tactics, e.g. pretending to grab it etc.

# The Shooting Gallery

## AIM

To get the group warmed up and to wake up
any dozers.

## EQUIPMENT

Chalk, a ball, coloured team bands (if you have
them).

## PREPARATION

A playing area as big as possible, laid out as
below.

| A Team | B Team | A Team | B Team |
|--------|--------|--------|--------|
| O | X X X | O O O | X |
| | X X X | O O O | |
| | X X X | O O O | |
| Firing Position | Shooting Gallery | | Firing Position |

- - - - - - - - - = chalk lines.
X = members of Team B
O = members of Team A

# HOW TO PLAY

1. The players take their place on the court as shown above with one member of each team outside the shooting gallery.

2. The single player from Team A has the ball to start with. (The ball can be a Sorbo Sponge, a football, a tennis ball etc., depending on the age and spread of the players.)

3. Player A throws the ball at Team B. If a member of Team B is hit by the ball, they are dead and join the single player outside the gallery. However, if they catch the ball they are not killed.

4. The ball passes rapidly between the courts with the numbers in the gallery reducing as they are hit in the crossfire.

5. The first team to eliminate all its opponents from the gallery is the winner.

# RULES

1. If a player is hit by the ball, whichever team threw it, that player must go to his/her side's firing position.

2. If a player catches the ball cleanly he/she is not out.

3. Players in the gallery can throw at the opposition in the gallery.

4. Players can pass the ball within their team.

**5.** Players cannot cross the chalk lines.

**6.** Balls must not be thrown at heads, but they can be thrown over the opponents' heads to your team behind them.

## HINTS

The game is fast and fun, and not as complicated as it seems.

# Sit On It

## AIM

An old favourite to get them moving.

## NUMBERS

From 4 to 400!

## EQUIPMENT

A pack of cards, one chair per person.

## HOW TO PLAY

1. Everyone sits on chairs in a circle.

2. Each person is given a playing card. They must note from this what suit they are for the rest of the game (hearts, clubs, diamonds or spades). The cards are then taken back and the leader shuffles the pack.

3. The leader turns over the top card and calls out the suit. Everyone whose card was that suit moves one seat to the right and, if there is someone there already, sits on their knee.

4. Another card is turned, and those with that suit move one seat to their right, unless they are being sat on, in which case they are unable to move.

**5.** The leader continues to call out suits quite quickly.

**6.** The winner is the first person to move all the way around the circle and return to his or her original seat (even if there is a pile of people already on it!).

## VARIATIONS

**1.** If the group is very small, have several laps.

**2.** Try having the red suits moving anti-clockwise and the blacks clockwise, just to complicate matters.

# Knight Riders

## AIM

A summer starter, best played outdoors.

## EQUIPMENT

String, small balloons filled with water.

## PREPARATION

Fill the balloons with water and tie a length of string to the end.

## HOW TO PLAY

1. Everyone finds a partner and mounts up 'piggy-back' style to mimic a knight and his horse. The knight is given a balloon on a length of string.

2. The object is to 'kill' other knights by hitting them with the water balloon so that it bursts on the opposing pair.

3. When a pair are wet, they are eliminated from the contest. The victor of the joust commandeers their water balloon and uses it to continue the battle.

4. If both balloons are burst simultaneously, both pairs are out.

**5.** The pair who remain at the end are the winners.

## HINTS

The amount of water in the balloons and their size are important. They should not be too heavy or the string too long. Do not let the contestants hit each other in the face with the balloons, as they can sting when they burst.

## VARIATIONS

If the group is large, this could become a team game.

# Chair Race

## AIM

Team building.

## EQUIPMENT

Five chairs per team.

## HOW TO PLAY

1. Divide the group into teams of six. Line the teams up behind a start line at one end of the hall, with their stack of five chairs behind them.

2. Mark off a finishing line at the other end of the hall.

3. Each team have to transport themselves and all the chairs from one end of the hall to the other without stepping on the floor between the start and finish lines. The chairs must not be moved by sliding; they can only be lifted and then placed. If a player touches the floor, he/she must return to the beginning.

4. The first team to have all its chairs stacked and to get all its members across the finish line wins.

# Robots

## HOW TO PLAY

1. Divide the group into two teams: One team are humanoid robots identical in every way to human beings, except that there has been a mistake in their programming. The other team are human investigators who are trying to locate the robots. Line the teams up opposite and facing each other.

2. The robots are each given a characteristics card with their personal characteristic written on it. They must thereafter obey the instruction on the card.

3. The investigators ask questions of the robots. Investigators have to take it in turns to ask questions and they can question any robot.

4. At any stage of the proceedings, an investigator may make a guess at what a robot's characteristic is. Investigators are even permitted to make a guess when it isn't their turn to question.

5. When a robot's characteristic has been guessed, that robot is eliminated.

6. Keep a score of how many questions each robot is asked before elimination and how many characteristics each investigator guesses.

**7.** The last robot remaining is the winner and the investigator who guesses the characteristic of the most robots also wins.

## CHARACTERISTICS

Here are some possible characteristics. Give each person on the robot team a card with one of these characteristics on it.

**1.** Just be yourself.
**2.** Always lie in the answers you give.
**3.** Always mention the name of a sweet in the answer.
**4.** Always mention a part of the body in your answer.
**5.** Always answer with another question.
**6.** Answer as if you were one of the leaders.
**7.** Always ask the questioner to repeat or clarify the question.
**8.** Always include the word 'Right' in your answer.
**9.** Always sniff when answering.
**10.** Avoid the question and don't answer it.
**11.** Always cross your legs while answering.
**12.** Always include a number in your answer.
**13.** Always refer to one of your parents while answering.

# Noughts and Crosses Relay

## AIM

Warm-up, ice-breaker.

## HOW TO PLAY

1. Lay out a grid of nine chairs as for a noughts and crosses game with about five feet between each chair, at one end of the hall.

2. Divide the group into two teams of equal numbers. Number the teams off, 1, 2, 3, 4, 5, 6 ... so that everyone has a number.

3. When you call out a number, the two players with that number race up the hall and sit on a seat. You keep calling numbers until a team has a row of three seats (as for noughts and crosses) or until all the seats are gone.

4. If a team gets a row they score 1 point. The first team to get 10 points is the winner.

## <u>VARIATIONS</u>

**1.** Call two numbers. The first has to piggy-back the second to the seat.

**2.** Have all of the team except one member blindfolded.

## <u>HINT</u>

Keep it moving fast.

# Ring of Knowledge

## AIM

Warm-up, to get them thinking as well as moving.

## HOW TO PLAY

Everyone sits on chairs in a circle, except one person, who stands in the middle. The object of the game is not to be in the middle. To get a seat the player in the middle asks any one person a question. This *must* be a 'Yes/No/ Don't know' question like 'Are you called Patrick?' rather than 'What is your name?' If the seated player answers 'Yes' everyone moves one seat to the right; if 'No' everyone moves one seat to the left; if 'I don't know' everyone runs across to the opposite chair in the circle. The player in the middle tries to get a seat while everyone is moving. If he/she succeeds, then the player left without a seat takes over in the middle.

## VARIATIONS

Questions could be set on a particular theme.

## HINT

Don't let the player in the middle get too near to the person he/she is asking a question.

# Body Dice

## AIM

Ice-breaker. This is a hit every time.

## EQUIPMENT

Materials for making two large dice.

## PREPARATION

Make two large dice. On one, number the sides 1 to 6. Label the other as follows: foot, elbow, head, armpit, hand, backside.

## HOW TO PLAY

1. Divide the group into teams of six, and number each person 1 to 6.

2. Both dice are rolled, and the number and part of the body are called out – e.g. number 2, armpit. Both dice are rolled again – e.g. number 4, elbow.

3. Now team member number 2 has to connect his/her armpit with number 4's elbow.

4. The two dice are thrown again twice, and another connection is made – e.g. number 5's hand to number 1's foot.

**5.** These connections are cumulative, so the groups get steadily more and more tangled. Eventually a group will not be able to make a connection – in which case they are out! The last group which is able to make a connection after the other group have failed is the winner.

## VARIATIONS

**1.** Change the body parts depending on the age/gender of the group.

**2.** It is possible to have groups of seven. When the same number is called twice – e.g. number 2, head to number 2, hand – the repeat number is called as a seven.

**3.** If you can't make two big dice, use two coloured dice with the numbers of one colour corresponding to body parts.

## HINT

Don't be too conservative! Kids will love this game and will want to play it again.

# Balloon Gladiators

## AIM

Warm-up.

## EQUIPMENT

Balloons, string.

## HOW TO PLAY

1. Divide the group into two equal teams.

2. The teams sit facing each other on a row of chairs and number off in pairs from left to right (starting from 1).

3. Each person is given a balloon and a piece of string. They blow the balloon up and tie it to their ankle with string.

4. A number is called out. The two people with that number must try to burst each other's balloon by stamping on it, at the same time protecting their own balloon from being burst.

5. The teams get a point for each surviving balloon. The team with the most points wins.

# VARIATIONS

1.  Call more than one number at once.

2.  Have replacement balloons and string so that players may have more than one go.

3.  Make the two gladiators hold either end of a rope loop in their left hands so that they are unable to run away from each other.

# Polo Mint Pass

## AIM

Fun, warm-up.

## EQUIPMENT

Two packets of Polos, cocktail sticks.

## HOW TO PLAY

1. Divide the group into two teams and give each person a cocktail stick.

2. Put an equal number of Polos on two chairs at the end of the hall.

3. Player one runs to the chair, puts the cocktail stick into his/her mouth and then, without using hands, picks up a Polo.

4. Players then return to their team and pass the Polo from cocktail stick to cocktail stick down the line (the sticks always being in players' mouths) without using their hands. The last player drops the Polo from the stick into a bowl and runs to the other end of the hall to pick up another Polo off the chair.

5. The first team to have all their Polos in the bowl are the winners.

# VARIATION

Introduce some obstacles for the Polo carriers to climb over or under.

# M & M Game

## AIM

Ice-breaker.

## EQUIPMENT

M & M's, straws, dishes.

## HOW TO PLAY

1. Divide the group into equal-sized teams. Give each player a straw.

2. Empty a packet of M & Ms into a dish on a table at the end of the hall.

3. The teams all line up at the end of the hall, one behind another.

**4.** The first person in each team runs to the dish, sucks up an M & M with the straw and runs back to the team.

**5.** The M & M is passed from straw to straw down the team by suction until it reaches the player at the back, who eats it off the straw.

**6.** The person who has eaten the M & M then runs to the dish and sucks up an M & M to pass back down the team in the same way.

**7.** The first team to have all eaten an M & M and to yell out 'M & Ms' is the winner.

## HINT

Use wide straws – old-fashioned 'school milk straws' – rather than narrow ones.

# Bumpy Ride

## AIM

To have fun.

## HOW TO PLAY

This is a great ice-breaker and never fails to be a great laugh. It needs 13 or more people for it to work.

Ask everyone to choose a partner. Then ask them to stand beside their partner, forming a double line down the centre of the room. Now ask everyone to lie on the floor on their backs, head to head touching their partner, and shoulder to shoulder touching the person beside them.

Ask them to put their hands in the air. Lower the odd person who is left over onto the raised hands of those lying on the floor. Then pass the person along the line.

## VARIATION

As a slightly more civilized variation you can use a mattress or an air-bed for the person to lie on.

# HINTS

If you have a small group, get each pair, when the person has passed over them, to get up and race to the end of the line so that you can keep the action continuously in motion. Then, when you reach the end of the hall or room, bring the person back again. Make sure that everyone lies close to each other, shoulders touching, or the support will collapse. It is best to choose someone who is not too heavy, and ask them to remove their shoes.

# Skittle Ball

## AIM

Fast-moving fun.

## EQUIPMENT

Tennis ball, chalk or masking tape, two empty two-litre plastic bottles.

## HOW TO PLAY

1.  Fill the two bottles one-third full of water (these will be the skittles).

2.  Position them at either end of the hall, three metres in from the end walls. With the chalk/masking tape mark a circle with a one-metre radius round each bottle.

3.  Divide the group into two teams and send the teams to either end of the hall.

4.  The object of the game is to knock over the opposing team's skittle with the tennis ball.

5.  Players cannot run with the ball; they cannot hold it for more than five seconds; they cannot touch other players; and, with the exception of the two goalkeepers, they cannot enter the circles around the skittles.

**6.** Each team chooses a goalkeeper who is allowed inside the circle to protect the skittle, but without touching it.

## SCORING

A team scores two points for knocking over the skittle with the ball. The opposition scores one point if the goalkeeper knocks over his/her own skittle.

## HINTS

Adjust the rules to suit the local conditions.

# Spaghetti Links

## AIM

Team-work, warm-up exercise.

## EQUIPMENT

One packet of spaghetti (not the wholewheat variety).

## PREPARATION

Partially cook the spaghetti.

## HOW TO PLAY

1. Divide the group into equal teams of between two and four members.

2. Give each team a bowl of the partially cooked spaghetti.

3. Each team has two minutes to construct the longest length of spaghetti string (made by tying the spaghetti lengths together).

4. The winners will be those with the longest length lifted off the ground by the ends, without it breaking.

# HINTS

The cooking time of the spaghetti is crucial for the desired effect. Practise with some individual strands before cooking it all.

**VOLUNTEERS ONLY**

# Spaghetti Numbers

## AIM

Fun and team-building.

## EQUIPMENT

Each of four volunteers will need: a bowl of spaghetti numbers, a piece of sugar-paper numbered 1 to 10 down the side, paper towels (optional), an old telephone directory and a list of ten people and/or organizations.

## HOW TO PLAY

Ask four volunteers to come to the front. Their task is to find the telephone numbers of the people/organizations by looking them up in the directory (it can be good to include numbers that might be useful for the young people to know, e.g. the youth leaders, the local police, the minister, Childline, etc.) and to write them out in spaghetti on the sugar-paper next to the corresponding number. The first to satisfactorily complete the task is the winner.

# Twin Cokes

## AIM

A fun, up-front game.

## EQUIPMENT

Two bottles of Coca-Cola (the traditional type) per contestant and some masking tape.

## PREPARATION

Tape each contestant's two bottles together around the widest part.

## HOW TO PLAY

Open the bottles and give them to the contestants. On the command 'Go!' they have to drink the contents of both the bottles, spilling as little as possible and not separating the two bottles. The winner is the first to successfully complete the task.

# Cold Feet

## AIM

Ice-breaker.

## EQUIPMENT

For each team: 10 marbles, 1 bucket/washing-up bowl, lots of ice and some water.

## PREPARATION

Freeze lots of ice-cubes and store in a freezer.

## HOW TO PLAY

1.  Volunteers come up to the front and sit on the chairs, then remove their shoes and socks.

2.  A bowl/bucket is brought in for each contestant, containing 10 marbles, lots of ice and a drop of water.

3.  The players have to remove the marbles using only their feet and without spilling the ice and water.

4.  The first player to remove all the marbles is the winner.

# **VARIATIONS**

Have the contestants blindfolded with a partner giving the 'fisher' instructions.

# Sumo Knights

## AIM

A lively opener which the lads will love as participants and the girls will like as spectators (or vice versa!).

## NUMBERS

Four or more.

## EQUIPMENT

Chalk and a suitable floor.

## PREPARATION

Draw a 15-foot-diameter circle on the floor with the chalk.

## HOW TO PLAY

1. The players need to be in pairs. Two pairs mount up piggy-back style and enter the circle. Each pair salutes the opposition by bowing 'sumo style'.
2. The object is either to knock over the opposition, thus scoring two points, or to knock them out of the circle, scoring one point. If either pair puts a foot outside the circle, the opposition wins a bonus point.

**3.** The first pair to get four points is the winner.

**4.** The contest ends with a ceremonial bow.

## HINTS

Don't let either of the pairs 'charge' their opposition, as this can be dangerous. It is advisable for any person wearing glasses to take them off.

## VARIATIONS

**1.** Team Sumo. Divide the group into two equal teams, and everyone has to do battle twice only. The team winning the most contests is the winner.

**2.** Tag Sumo. As above, except the pair in the circle can tag another pair from their team who are waiting on the edge of the circle and then swap over. This gives a continuous battle, as in tag wrestling.

# Spaghetti Hairdo

## AIM

Up-front ice-breaker.

## EQUIPMENT

Three chairs, three bowls, some cooked spaghetti.

## PREPARATION

Cook the spaghetti.

## HOW TO PLAY

1.  Ask for three male volunteers and ask them to come and sit down on the chairs.

2.  Explain that none of the lads has a trendy hairdo and that you would like three girls to come and restyle their hair.

3.  When the girls are in place, bring out the bowls of spaghetti and explain that the girls have to restyle the lads' hair (putting the spaghetti actually on the lads' heads).

4.  Give them three minutes to construct a hair-style and get the rest of the group to judge the winner.

5.  Give the winner a prize (hair gel?).

# Worm Slurp

## AIM

A screaming start to the evening.

## EQUIPMENT

Liquorice strings, of the same or of differing lengths. Four bowls of chocolate instant whip (or use just one bowl).

## PREPARATION

Place the liquorice strings in the bottom of the bowl, leaving one end of each string visible over the edge, and pour in the runny instant whip.

## HOW TO PLAY

1.  Choose four volunteers, either by encouragement or by bribery!

2.  Explain that the first person to eat the liquorice string will win a prize, be a Mega Star for the evening, etc.

3.  The contestants position themselves next to an end of liquorice string and on the command 'Go' start chewing the string without using their hands.

**4.** The winner is the first person to eat the string.

# HINTS

**1.** If your group meets in your lounge, it might be a good idea to protect the carpet with a plastic sheet.

**2.** The consistency of the instant whip must not be too solid or too runny.

# VARIATIONS

Blindfold the contestants and use differing lengths of liquorice. With lots of cheering and group noise, the last contestant will not realize that he or she is chewing away alone. Use this as a discussion starter on deception or being the odd one out.

# Blindfold Identikit

## AIM

This is a great up-front game.

## EQUIPMENT

A blindfold, five washing-up bowls, a can of baked beans, a packet of cornflakes, some ice, some marbles, some maggots, a towel for washing feet afterwards.

## HOW TO PLAY

1. Three volunteers are brought out to the front and taken backstage into a side room, out of sight. Ask them to remove one shoe and one sock.

2. One at a time they are brought in blindfolded and sat in a chair. The bowls are then placed in front of them, one at a time, and the contestants have to identify the contents by feeling them with their feet.

3. The player who correctly identifies the most (or the one who screams the loudest when they realize that their feet are in a bowl of maggots!) is the winner.

## SOURCE

Thanks to our friends at the local Assemblies
of God church for this game.

# Water Laser Quest

## AIM

A wet up-front game. The audience are in danger as well!

## EQUIPMENT

Blindfolds (optional), 'targets' made from brightly coloured card, masking tape, two water-pistols.

## HOW TO PLAY

1. Two superhero/heroine volunteers are brought to the front and suitably attired for the game. Targets are stuck to their front and back with masking tape.

2. The audience are then invited to scream support for each champion in turn.

3. The contestants are then given a water-pistol each. They now fire at each other, and the first one to score a hit on one of the other's targets is the winner. (For extra laughs, the two contestants could be blindfolded!)

## HINT

If you are using pump-action, high-volume water pistols, be prepared for everyone to get wet!

# Balloon Hugging

## AIM

Up-front fun.

## EQUIPMENT

Balloons.

## HOW TO PLAY

1.  Couples or potential couples (or even complete strangers who look like likely victims!) are invited up to the front.

2.  Each couple stand toe to toe, staring into each other's eyes (or, if you get it wrong, staring over the head and into the neck of each other!).

3.  The couples are then given a balloon, which is placed between the two of them. The aim of the game is to pop the balloon as quickly as possible by hugging each other. No contact with the balloon is allowed with hands, teeth etc.

4.  The first couple to burst the balloon are the winners.

# The Jelly Baby Game

## AIM

To encourage sharing, as a discussion starter for looking at privilege, Third-World needs etc.

## EQUIPMENT

Jelly babies (lots).

## PREPARATION

Buying the equipment.

## HOW TO PLAY

The group should all be seated and each person is given about 20 jelly babies. Then, starting with the youngest, each person shares with the group one thing they have never done which they would like to do, e.g. visit France, have a brother/sister, live in the countryside. After a person has shared, all those people who have done the thing have to give that person a jelly baby. When everyone has had a chance to share something with the group, see who has the most jelly babies and who has the least.

# VARIATIONS

1.  If the group is very small, then it would be
    worth having several rounds of sharing. If the
    group is very large, then it might be better to
    split into smaller groups.

2.  There are a number of categories about which
    people could share, e.g.:
    - 'I wish I had a ...' – material possessions.
    - 'I wish I was able to ...' – talents and abilities.

# HINTS

Prevent it from becoming a competition
- by your attitude as a leader.
- by the atmosphere of the room.

# If I Were ...

## AIM

A non-competitive discussion-starter.

## EQUIPMENT

None.

## PREPARATION

None.

## HOW TO PLAY

1.  Set up the room so that the seats are facing each other and a friendly atmosphere is created to encourage sharing.

2.  Name a category, e.g. Animal.

3.  In turns, everyone says, 'If I were an animal, I would be a ...' If they wish they can explain the reason for their choice.

4.  The group should be quiet while people speak, but questions may be asked when they have finished.

# <u>VARIATIONS</u>

Use any number of categories: e.g. flowers, trees, houses, shops, people.

# <u>HINTS</u>

Try to ensure that people share what they *are* like and not what they *want* to be like. Or you may decide to do both together: 'If I were an animal, I would be …' and 'If I were an animal, I would like to be …'

# Did You Know?

## AIM

To deepen relationships within the group.

## EQUIPMENT

Pen and paper for everyone.

## HOW TO PLAY

This is an extremely simple activity which is usually very amusing. The time taken depends on the size of your group – it can take up to 40 minutes with a group of 20.

1.  Ask them to write down six relatively unknown facts about themselves. They may need a bit of prompting, so suggest things such as their favourite colour, pop group, TV personality, breakfast cereal or TV programme. You could also suggest things like places they have visited, people they have met or unusual things they have done. Allow about 10 minutes. Some may need to be encouraged to think hard, but make sure they put down six facts. Ask them not to put their names on the papers.

2.  Now ask them to fold up their paper into a fairly small piece. Collect each piece of paper in a container.

**3.** This is where the fun begins. Ask someone to select one of the pieces of paper and to read out slowly the six facts written down. As they are reading out the list, ask the group to guess who the facts apply to. When the person has been found, ask him/her to pick the next piece of paper.

## HINTS

This activity does not work so well with a very young teenage group, so you could ask them to think of four facts instead of six. Take care that the activity does not consume too much of your time in the evening's programme. Sometimes it can go on a lot longer than you expect.

# Road Map

## AIM

To deepen relationships within the group.

## EQUIPMENT

A pen and a large piece of paper for each person.

## HOW TO PLAY

1.  Give each person a large piece of paper and a pen. Tell them to draw a very small square in the bottom right-hand corner, then a similar square in the top-left hand corner. The first square at the bottom of the page represents the day they were born and the square at the top is today.

2.  Now get them to draw a map of their life beginning at birth, asking them to represent pictorially any significant event along the way, e.g. a stay in hospital, their first school, places they have visited or lived in. Allow plenty of time and encourage them to be artistic – even those who claim they cannot draw.

3.  When everyone has finished, put them in pairs with people they do not know very well, and then ask them to explain to each other

what they have drawn. This can be a very valuable activity, and often people discover some significant things about other people. It is a non-threatening way of getting people to open up and begin to relate to each other in a deeper way.

## VARIATIONS

After people have accomplished the activity in pairs, you can either ask them to change partners or divide them up into groups of four.

## HINTS

This activity tends to work better with older teenagers, although with some encouragement it can work well with younger ones.

# More Fat than Thin

## AIM

Thought-provoking warm-up.

## EQUIPMENT

None.

## PREPARATION

Construct a list as below.

## HOW TO PLAY

**1.** Everyone stands in the middle of the room and the leader asks, 'Are you more happy than sad?' and points to one end of the room which is then designated 'sad' and then to the other end which is designated 'happy'.

**2.** The young people have to choose which end it would be most appropriate for them to stand at, and then they move to it. There is no standing in the middle.

**3.** Then call out another pair of characteristics – e.g. more fat than thin – and again, they have to choose and move to one end of the room. Other calls could include:
- loner/crowd-seeker
- quiet/noisy

- beautiful/ugly
- extrovert/introvert
- thinker/doer
- local/foreign
- Christian/non-Christian

**4.** When the young people have got the hang of it, allow them to challenge other people's positions – e.g. 'You're not fat', 'You should be at this end' etc.

**5.** End with discussion, asking if people were surprised by the ways in which others perceived them.

# Crazy God Quiz

## HOW TO PLAY

Give every member of the group a question-naire like the one overleaf. This is in the form of a star profile as found in teen magazines. For the 'God File' the young people need to imagine who God's favourite band would be, what his favourite food would be and so on.

The results will vary, depending on age and culture, but the young people's choices will always say something about how they view God, even if these choices seem trivial.

When they have filled in the quiz sheet, share the answers around the group.

## Crazy God Quiz

If I had to give God a colour, it would be.....................
Why?............................
.......................................

*The God File*

Fave band

What God likes best about me is.............................
Why?............................
.......................................

Fave food

Best moment

My favourite bit of God's Book is........................
.......................................

The person he is most pleased he created

God influences how much of my life? Circle the nearest answer:
0% 5% 10% 20%
30% 40% 50% 60%
70% 80% 90% 100%

Most likely to say

God makes me feel........
.......................................

One question I have always wanted to ask God is......
.......................................
.......................................

Least likely to say

## I Am ... You Are ...

## AIM

To encourage the group members to express how they feel about each other, and to be open and honest about strengths and weaknesses.

## WARM-UP

If your group enjoys singing, then some quiet worship songs or a Taizé chant would be good. If not, use a Christian meditation or a relaxation exercise – something that will quieten them and turn their thoughts towards God.

## MAIN ACTIVITY

1. Tape a piece of A4 paper to each person's back and give them each a soft pencil or felt pen.

2. Ask each person to write on the back of all the others one thing they like about them.

3. Sit round in a circle, remove the papers, and get everyone to read out their list. They should say, 'I am ...' if they agree with what is written, or 'Someone says I am ...' if they don't agree.

4. Spend a time of quiet reflecting on this.

**5.** Stick another piece of paper on everyone's backs, and ask the group to write one thing they dislike about each person on the sheet.

**6.** Sit round in a circle. Again everyone reads their list, saying, 'I am ...' if they agree, or 'Someone says I am ...' if they disagree.

**7.** Spend some time quietly reflecting.

**8.** Ask each person in turn how they feel.

**9.** Then ask the group to pray for each person, either quietly or aloud.

## HINTS

If the group is too large, break it down into smaller units and hold the session in different rooms.

If you do this activity you need to be confident that the group can handle it, and you need to exercise the utmost care and sensitivity.

# Can I Help?

## AIM

A quiet warm-up.

## EQUIPMENT

Problem cards.

## PREPARATION

Write out some problem cards. For example:

1.  You are an elderly lady whose garden is overgrown now that your husband is dead.

2.  Your boyfriend has packed you in.

3.  You have been sacked from your Saturday job.

4.  You want to give up smoking.

5.  You are lonely.

6.  Your parents do not like your friends.

7.  [Add your own.]

# HOW TO PLAY

1. One person takes one of the problem cards at random. The rest of the group has to ask questions to find out what the problem is.

2. Questions can only be answered 'Yes' or 'No'.

3. Each person is allowed a maximum of three questions, and then one guess at what the problem is.

4. Individuals score one point per problem guessed correctly.

# Mirrors

## AIM

A gentle trust game.

## HOW TO PLAY

1. Everyone finds a partner. (If there is an uneven number, pair one person with a leader.)

2. Ask them to label themselves 'A' or 'B'.

3. Tell the pairs to stand a pace apart, with arms out, palms almost touching, so that 'B' is the mirror of 'A'.

4. 'A' slowly moves his/her arms and body, and 'B' has to follow as accurately as possible, without ever touching.

5. Repeat, but with 'B' leading and 'A' following.

**GROUP BUILDERS**

# Lost on the Moon

## AIM

Teamwork, decision-making and consensus-seeking.

## EQUIPMENT

Photocopied 'Lost on the Moon' sheets, copies of the NASA Rankings, pencils.

## HOW TO PLAY

1.  Divide the group into smaller units of between five and seven members.

2.  Each person is given a copy of the 'Lost on the Moon' sheet. The task is to rank each item in order of importance for the group's survival. (It is important that, initially, this is done individually.)

# Lost on the Moon!

Your spaceship has just crashed on the Moon. You are scheduled to rendezvous with a mother ship 200 miles away on the lighted side of the Moon, but the rough landing has ruined your ship and destroyed all the equipment on board, except for the 15 items listed below. Your crew's survival depends on reaching the mother ship, so you must choose the most critical items for the 200-mile trip. Your task is to rank the items in order of their importance for survival. Write '1' by the most important item and '15' by the least important.

_____ Box of matches
_____ Food concentrate
_____ 50 feet of nylon rope
_____ Parachute silk
_____ Solar-powered portable heater
_____ 2 .45-calibre pistols
_____ 1 case of dehydrated milk
_____ 2 100-pound tanks of oxygen
_____ Stellar map of the Moon's constellations
_____ Self-inflating life-raft
_____ Magnetic compass
_____ 5 gallons of water
_____ Signal flares
_____ First-aid kit containing injection needles
_____ Solar-powered FM receiver-transmitter

**3.** After everyone has completed the list, the small groups now have to draw up a corporate list which they all agree about.

**4.** When the group lists are done, pass out the NASA result sheets and ask everyone to score how well they did, first as individuals and then as a group.

**5.** The individuals and groups find their error marks by calculating the difference between their ranking of any particular item and NASA's. For survival, the error ratio must be less than 20.

**6.** Discussion together:
- Which individuals survived and which did not?
- Which groups survived?
- Were the group surprised by any of the rankings?
- Which ones and why?
- How did each group decide what their priorities were?
- Was this different from the way in which individuals decided the same thing?
- What was done in the groups with those members who disagreed with the group list?
- Who was the leader? etc.

# Lost on the Moon: Solution

| Items | NASA's reasoning | NASA's ranks | Your ranks | Error points |
|---|---|---|---|---|
| Box of matches | No oxygen on Moon to sustain flame. | 15 | | |
| Food concentrate | Efficient means of supplying energy. | 4 | | |
| Nylon rope | Useful in scaling cliffs, tying injured together. | 6 | | |
| Parachute silk | Protection from sun rays. | 8 | | |
| Portable heater | Not needed unless on the dark side. | 13 | | |
| Pistols | Possible means of self-propulsion. | 11 | | |
| Dehydrated milk | Bulkier duplication of food concentrate. | 12 | | |
| Oxygen tanks | Most pressing survival need. | 1 | | |
| Stellar map | Primary means of navigation. | 3 | | |
| Self-inflating life-raft | $CO_2$ bottle in military raft may be used for propulsion. | 9 | | |
| Magnetic compass | Magnetic field on Moon is not polarized; worthless for navigation. | 14 | | |
| 5 gallons of water | Replacement for tremendous liquid loss on lighted side. | 2 | | |
| Signal flares | Distress signal when mother ship is sighted. | 10 | | |
| First-aid kit | Needles for medicine etc. will fit into special aperture in NASA space suits. | 7 | | |
| Solar-powered FM receiver-transmitter | For communication with mother ship; but FM requires line-of-sight transmission and short ranges. | 5 | | |

# The Square Game

## AIM

Teamwork discussion exercise.

## PREPARATION

Lay out a court measuring three metres by three metres, containing nine squares with one-metre sides. Prepare numbered cards and the solution sheet to put on the wall.

## EQUIPMENT

The solution sheet (see below), cards numbered 1 to 8, paper and pencils.

## MAIN ACTIVITY

1. Lay out numbered cards in the court in the following pattern:

| 7 | 1 | 3 |
|---|---|---|
| 2 |   | 5 |
| 6 | 4 | 8 |

**2.** Put the solution sheet on the wall:

| 1 | 2 | 3 |
|---|---|---|
| 4 | 5 | 6 |
| 7 | 8 |   |

**3.** Brief the group as follows. Eight players are needed. Each of them should stand in one of the squares containing a numbered card. The task is for the group to rearrange the players to conform to the solution sheet, but these rules must be followed:

- No talking.
- Players can step forwards, backwards or sideways.
- No one can move diagonally.
- Players can move only into an empty space.
- Only one player can be in any one square at a time.
- Cards may not be exchanged.
- Players may not move out of the grid.
- Those who are not playing should be given paper and pencils to observe those who are.

**4.** On the order to start, the group should begin to work towards the solution. Allow them about 20 minutes in silence, and then, if they show little sign of completing the task, allow them to talk.

**5.** After 40 minutes, or when the task has been completed, gather everyone around to debrief and to discuss the activity.

## DEBRIEF

1. Who moved first and how did they decide to move?

2. How were the moves organized?

3. Did people use non-verbal communication? How?

4. Did people use verbal communication?

5. Was everyone aware of everyone else's number?

6. Who felt frustrated, annoyed etc.? Why?

7. Who facilitated and who blocked the task?

## GOING FURTHER

What is the task of a Christian youth group? What facilitates or blocks that task?

# Lego Towers

## AIM

A team-work exercise.

## PREPARATION

Photocopy some points-scoring sheets, instructions and graphs.

## EQUIPMENT

Bags of 350 Lego bricks (size 4x2), points-scoring sheets, instructions and graphs.

## HOW TO PLAY

1.  Divide the group into teams of four and pos-ition the teams out of sight of each other.

2.  Give each team a copy of the instructions and a points-scoring sheet. Then let them play!

3.  After the towers are built, measure them, count up the bricks and the time and calculate the winner.

4.  Discuss together:
    *   Who was the leader?
    *   How did the group work together?
    *   Was everyone included?

- What hindered the task?
- Why did some teams do better than others?

---

## Instructions

**1.** You are to build a tower which scores maximum points (see graphs).

**2.** The tower must be self-supporting.

**3.** You have 25 minutes to plan the tower and a maximum of 10 minutes to build it.

**4.** During the planning stage you may assemble bricks, but these must be detached before the building phase.

**5.** On completion the points scored will be calculated, and the team scoring the most is the winner.

---

## Points-scoring sheet (refer to graphs)

Height (cm)..................... Score..........................
No. of bricks................... Score..........................
Time (mins)..................... Score..........................
Total score...........................................................

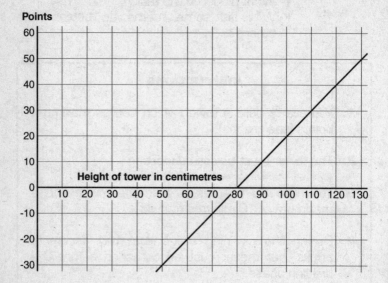

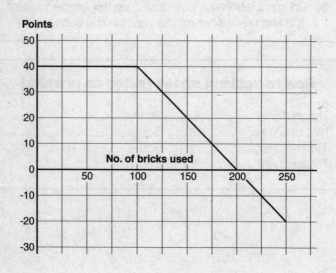

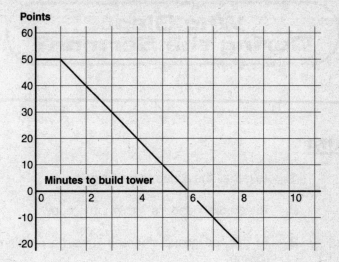

# Who Slept During the Sermon?

## AIM

**1.** To get all the group to participate.

**2.** To establish leaders within the group.

**3.** To get the group oriented towards problem solving.

## PREPARATION

Write each of the 20 clues on a separate piece of paper.

## MAIN ACTIVITY

Give the group the following information (adapting the leadership titles to your group's church background):

During a lengthy sermon by the Vicar, one of the churchwardens is noticed to be asleep. Twenty members of the congregation each gave the Vicar one piece of information concerning the suspect. Unfortunately the Vicar was unable to work out who was asleep. We have here all the information needed to find out who it was.

# Clues

1. The man in the black coat smiled.
2. The man in the blue coat sat behind the man in the black coat.
3. Mr Turner never frowned during sermons.
4. Mr Bouch never smiled during sermons.
5. Mr McWhirr would never wear black to church.
6. Mr Turner sat on the right of the man in the brown coat.
7. Mr McWhirr was always early for church.
8. Mr Bouch sat behind the man in the grey coat.
9. The man in the grey coat sat in front of the man in the blue coat.
10. The man in the grey coat listened throughout the sermon.
11. Mr Lumb had spilled coffee down his only grey coat and it was at the dry cleaners.
12. The man who frowned sat to the left of the man who slept.
13. The Vicar could never see those at the back from the pulpit.
14. The man who slept wore a hat.
15. The man who slept sat behind the man in grey.
16. Mr Turner wore his black coat only for funerals.
17. The man who slept sat on the right of the man in the brown coat.
18. Mr McWhirr sat behind the man in the grey suit.
19. The man in the black suit did not sit behind Mr Bouch.
20. Mr Bouch sat to the left of the man in the blue coat.

# Rules

1. Everyone will be given a clue or clues.
2. No one can look at anyone else's clues.
3. The only way to share your clue is by speaking.
4. We will only tell you if the answer is right or wrong.

# Solution

*Blue*
McWhirr
SLEPT

*Grey*
Turner
Listened

*Brown*
Bouch
Frowned

*Black*
Lumb
Smiled

# DISCUSSION

When the group have solved the problem, discuss the following points:

**1.** Was a leader needed?
**2.** How was time lost?
**3.** Why was it least effective for everyone to talk at once?
**4.** What problems arose because some people did not present their clues?
**5.** How did some people ignore the clues of others?
**6.** Did anyone try to encourage everyone to give their clues?
**7.** Was everyone included in the discussion?
**8.** Did anyone take over the discussion?

# The Parable of the Talents

## AIM

To teach a biblical parable in the memorable way and to raise funds for the youth group.

## EQUIPMENT

Paper, pencils, Bibles, questions, envelopes numbered 1 to 4 containing different amounts of money: £10, £5, £2, £1.

## MAIN ACTIVITY

1. Divide the youth group into groups of four or five, including those who are absent, so that every member is included in a team.

2. Tell them that each group will be given an envelope containing an amount of money (for greater impact use your own money if you can afford it). They have to use it to its best advantage and make the most profit with it. Tell them that in a few weeks' time (but do not specify exactly when) you will call them to account for what they have done.

3. Each group chooses a number and receives the envelope with that number on. They can open the envelope and see how much money

they have to spend. They then have to plan how they are going to use the money most profitably, write down their action plan and hand it in.

**4.** When all the groups have done this, tell them that no one will know when they will be called to account, then play an appropriate ice-breaker.

## FOLLOW-UP

**1.** Six weeks later, ask the young people to get back into their teams and choose one person from each team to report back to the whole group on how they used the money and if they made any profit.

**2.** When all the groups have reported, congratu-late them on how well they did. Give them a Bible and a question sheet and ask them to answer the questions in their group.

**3.** When the groups have finished and reported back, give everyone a piece of paper. Ask them to write on it any talents they would like God to use in their lives that have so far been unused. If they would like to use these talents in the youth group or in church, ask them to hand them in.

**4.** Close with prayers.

**5.** After the meeting is over, pray for those who have handed in talent papers, and with your church leaders discuss how their gifts can be used in church.

# Questions

1. Read Matthew 25:14–30.
2. Are there any similarities between the parable and the exercise that you have done?
3. Which of the groups was like which of the servants in the parable?
4. When Jesus is talking about talents, is he talking about money?
5. If not, then what is he talking about?
6. What talents do you feel you do not use as God intended?

# Air Crash Survival

## AIM

Team-building and decision-making exercise.

## EQUIPMENT

Enough photocopied sheets of the 'Survival Situation' for one person plus one per group, and also enough copies of the 'Survival Items Priority List' for one per person.

## HOW TO PLAY

1.  This is similar to 'Lost on the Moon'. Each person is given a copy of the 'Survival Situation' and has to rank the 15 items in order of their importance for survival. After everyone has completed their own priority list, divide the group into small teams to produce team priority lists, allowing plenty of time for them to come to a consensus – i.e. everyone must agree with the decisions taken, without having to vote or one person dominating the choice etc.

2.  When the teams have produced their lists, give everyone a copy of the 'Survival Items Priority List' to see how well they have done and whether or not they think they would have actually survived.

# Survival Situation

The plane in which you were travelling has crashed – you and your group are the only survivors. The plane was well off course so you do not know where you are.

The terrain you were flying over was thick woodland crossed by numerous rivers and lakes. At this time of year the temperature will be minus 25° in the daytime and minus 40° at night. The time is now 11 a.m.

You have managed to rescue the 15 items listed below. Your task is to rank the items in order of their priority for your survival. Number them 1 to 15 (1 is the most important and 15 is the least). You have decided to stay together at the crash site. Apart from the 15 items listed below and the clothes you are wearing (winter wear appropriate to a town), everything else and the plane has been burnt up or destroyed.

| Rank | Items |
|------|-------|
| _____ | Compress kit (10m of 5cm gauze) |
| _____ | Ball of steel wool |
| _____ | Cigarette lighter (no fuel) |
| _____ | Loaded .45 calibre pistol |
| _____ | Newspapers (1 per person) |
| _____ | Magnetic compass |
| _____ | Two ski poles |
| _____ | Knife |
| _____ | Sectional air map made of plastic |
| _____ | 30 feet of rope |
| _____ | Family-sized chocolate bar (1 per person) |
| _____ | Torch with batteries |
| _____ | Bottle of 85 % proof whisky |
| _____ | Extra clothing (for each survivor) |
| _____ | Can of lard |

# Survival Items Priority List

1. **Cigarette lighter** — A positive task such as lighting a fire would help to counteract the effect of shock and would also give warmth. The lighter is the source of the spark to light the fire.

2. **Ball of steel wool** — This will hold a spark to help get the fire established.

3. **Extra clothing** — Warmth.

4. **Chocolate bar** — Food.

5. **Can of lard** — Has insulation properties. Can be made into candles. Will help to light the fire. Can be eaten. The empty container could also be used.

6. **Torch with batteries** — Use as a signal light. Torch batteries will ignite the steel wool to start the fire.

7. **30 feet of rope** — Can be used in the building of a shelter and for fishing. Can be burnt on the fire as fuel if dry. Use for candle wicks.

8. **Newspaper** — Will provide insulation, reading material and toilet paper.

9. **Loaded .45 calibre pistol** — Can be used for hunting and signalling. Powder from the bullets could make an explosive charge.

10. **Knife** — Hunting, carving, skinning etc.

11. **Compress kit** — First aid, protection, tinder for the fire.

12. **Two ski poles** — To make heat reflector to keep heat in. Use in the shelter or to make a stretcher.

13. **Bottle of whisky** — For the fire.

14. **Sectional air map** — Insulation for one person only.

15. **Magnetic compass** — Not much use, as nobody is going anywhere.

**3.** The important thing is to talk about how the group worked in their decision-making process. How well did the group listen to individuals' thoughts and feelings? How defensive were individuals about their own points of view? Who was the most persuasive? Who gave way most often?

# Arrows

## EQUIPMENT

Four A4 sheets of blue paper with a large arrow on each, and four red pieces of paper with a large arrow on each.

## PREPARATION

Produce a copy of the Instruction Sheet for each team.

## ACTION

Note the starting time and make sure that no cheating goes on. If the rules need clarifying, help them out, but otherwise see how long it takes. It could be 30 seconds or 30 minutes!

# Instruction Sheet

**1.** Note the starting position of your arrows. This is where they have to be returned to if you want to start again.

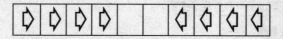

**2.** The task is to move all the red arrows to the blue end and all the blue arrows to the red end.

**3.** There are only two possible moves:
   (a) an arrow can move one space forward if the space in front is empty;
   (b) an arrow can hop forwards over an arrow of the opposite colour.

**4.** The following moves are not permitted:
   (a) to move backwards;
   (b) to move into an occupied space;
   (c) to hop over more than one opposing arrow at once;
   (d) to hop over an arrow of the same colour.

**5.** The team that can complete the task in the quickest time is the winner.

# The Great Youth Group Disaster

## AIM

To work together as a group on problem solving.

## PREPARATION

Photocopy the 'Key facts' and cut the paper into strips so that each fact is on an individual strip of paper.

## THE GENERAL SCENE

It's Monday morning and the Youth Minister has discovered that the video, the TV and all the Mars Bars are missing from the club. He rings all the youth leaders to find out what they have to say, but owing to an extremely bad line, he only gets down part of what they all said.

The Pastor has asked the Youth Minister to come to him and explain in an hour's time, and he has already used up half an hour writing up the 'Key facts'.

## THE TASK

Your task is to try to work out what happened on Sunday night, and how the place was robbed without any sign of a forced entry.

- Each person will be given a number of 'Key facts'.
- You cannot show your pieces of paper to anyone.
- You can only share their contents by reading them out to the group.
- You have 30 minutes to solve the mystery.

## KEY FACTS

1. There were five leaders on duty on Sunday night.
2. Each leader had a different responsibility.
3. Only the two section leaders had keys.
4. The two senior leaders had sole responsibility for locking up.
5. There was only one male senior leader.
6. The fire exit, when closed, could only be opened from the inside.
7. The kitchen hatch was closed when the club was closed.
8. The youth club had three exits.
9. The main exit leads onto Old Church Road.
10. The church front door had to be opened and closed with a key.
11. The door from the club to the church could be opened from the club side, without a key.
12. The leader who washed up left third at 10.15 p.m.
13. One person let himself or herself out through the church.
14. Hannah's car was parked on the Main Street until 10.10 p.m.
15. The tuckshop cashier drove home first.
16. The leader who washed up left through the fire exit.
17. Two leaders chatted in the kitchen about the evening until 10.20 p.m.

18. David was home before the late movie started. It started at 10.15 p.m.
19. Someone re-entered through the main exit to collect their coat.
20. John was the last to drive home.
21. It took five minutes for the leader who washed up to find his coat in church.
22. The leader who tidied the games equipment never wore a coat.
23. A senior leader checked the club and locked the main door as he left.
24. Peter left through the main exit.
25. Two people used the fire exit.
26. Only two leaders drove to church.
27. Rebecca usually went for a run after club.
28. The leader who tidied the games equipment left through the fire exit.
29. Peter left the door open when he left.

## CORRECT SOLUTION

Peter washed up and then left through the main exit at 10.15 p.m. He returned to the club to find his coat, which was in church. By the time he had found his coat, the club had been locked up and everyone had gone. He left through the fire exit and forgot to shut it properly.

## DEBRIEFING

If the group have found a solution, tell them if it is correct and move on to the debriefing. If their solution is not the correct one, either give them a little more time or explain what the situation is before moving on to the debriefing:

- How do you feel?
- How did the group go about completing the task?
- Who did what in the group?
- Who took the lead?
- Who hindered the result?
- Who was the quietest person?
- What was necessary for the puzzle to be solved?
- Were any assumptions made in finding the solution?
- How can we apply the process of puzzle solving to this group?

## GOING FURTHER

In reality, the removal of some of the material possessions of the youth club is not such a disaster. There are other things, however, that could happen that would be a real youth group disaster.

- What would be a real disaster for this group?
- What action could we or should we take after the disaster?
- Are there disasters happening already that we do not see?
- What was the biggest disaster in Jesus' life and ministry? Why?

# 24-Hour Dilemma

## AIM

To look at how the young people would cope in certain situations.

## EQUIPMENT

A Dilemma Board (see below), a set of Dilemma Cards (ditto), dice, counters etc. (If the group is large you may need two sets of equipment.)

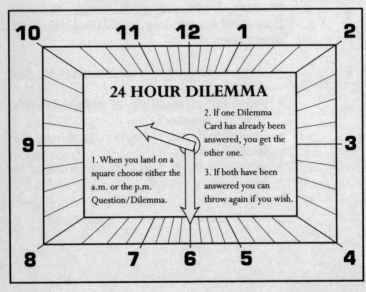

10   11   12   1   2

**24 HOUR DILEMMA**

2. If one Dilemma Card has already been answered, you get the other one.

1. When you land on a square choose either the a.m. or the p.m. Question/Dilemma.

3. If both have been answered you can throw again if you wish.

9   3

8   7   6   5   4

# HOW TO PLAY

1. Each player needs a token. They can start from any time in the day or night.

2. The object is to cope with any crisis that you encounter.

3. The player throws the dice and moves the number of hours round the board indicated by the dice.

4. The player turns up and reads the appropriate Dilemma Card for the hour.

5. The player has to say what he/she would do in that situation.

6. When the player has finished, the other players can challenge what he/she has said in two ways:
   (a) They can say that the action which he/she has taken is the incorrect action for that situation.
   (b) They can say that it is not the action which the individual would take in the situation.

7. When the person has replied to the challenge, move on to the next player.

8. The game ends when time runs out or when all the situations have been dealt with.

# DILEMMA CARDS

7 a.m.        While on your paper round you notice that you are being followed by an unknown man.

8 a.m.        In your reading this morning from the Old Testament, God slays Israel's enemies, and you can't understand why God would do something like that.

9 a.m.        You were out late the night before and you know that if you don't get up now you won't make it to church.

10 a.m.      At school someone in your class is being bullied. You don't particularly like them, but what should you do?

11 a.m.      While in town you find a wallet with over £50 in it. What should you do?

Noon         While cooking lunch you burn your hand on the cooker. No one else is home.

1 p.m.        You want to start a lunchtime Christian meeting at school, but you haven't got a room to meet in.

2 p.m.        While out clothes shopping with a friend he/she wants to buy something outrageous/provocative/expensive.

3 p.m.        Some of your friends are meeting down at the arcade for an afternoon of video games.

4 p.m.        A group of friends meet for a smoke after school and invite you along.

| | |
|---|---|
| 5 p.m. | You're in a burger bar and one of your friends won't eat or drink anything. You realize that it's weeks since you have seen them eating. |
| 6 p.m. | The youth group are holding a barbecue but you are meant to be having tea with your grandparents. |
| 7 p.m. | One of your acquaintances from school has asked you to take him/her to the youth group, but they are not part of the crowd. |
| 8 p.m. | You have some homework that has to be in the next day, but you would rather be doing something else. |
| 9 p.m. | Your parents are out and you are making yourself a cup of tea, when you smell gas in the kitchen. |
| 10 p.m. | Your friends are all staying late at a party but you promised that you would be home at 10 p.m. |
| 11 p.m. | A friend comes round really upset because his/her parents are arguing and fighting again. |
| Midnight | You are at a sleepover when your friends decide to watch a video meant for adults only. |
| 1 a.m. | Mum and Dad went out for a quick drink down the pub and haven't got back yet. |
| 2 a.m. | You hear your Mum in tears because it would have been your Dad's birthday, but he died last year. |

| 3 a.m. | You wake up because your little brother is being sick. Mum's on the night shift and you know Dad has to be up early for work. |
|---|---|
| 4 a.m. | You wake up frightened by nightmares and you can't get back to sleep. |
| 5 a.m. | Your older sister/brother, with whom you share a room, has an asthma attack. |
| 6 a.m. | You wake early and are watching the dawn when you see a man climbing out of a nearby house's window. |

# Egg Launch

## EQUIPMENT

Ten garden canes, a funnel, some string, two eggs and any other things that might be helpful.

## PREPARATION

Collect the equipment and write out an Instruction Card.

## ACTION

Give each team a copy of the Instruction Card overleaf. It is best to play this game outside.

## HINTS

The eggs will travel a wide range of distances (one group managed 12 metres!), so don't fire towards your car or your church!

# Instruction Card

**1.** Your team's task is to produce an egg launcher using as much of the equipment as you wish.

**2.** Your team has 30 minutes in which to build its launch mechanism, after which the leaders will bring you a real egg to launch. The one with the equipment is your practice egg.

**3.** The launcher must be self-standing, i.e. it cannot be stuck in the ground or held by the team in any way.

**4.** The launch of the egg cannot involve any input of energy from the person launching. You can release something, but you can't push or pull something.

**5.** When the egg is launched, the distance measured is from the front of the machine to where the egg lands.

**6.** The team firing an egg the longest distance wins.

# Group Friendship Sculpture

## AIM

To help the young people understand where they are in relationship to their friends, or to look at spiritual snobbery, or to look at families or childhood.

## WARM-UP

Sharing games.

## EQUIPMENT

Pens and paper.

## MAIN ACTIVITY

1. Ask for a volunteer to stand in the middle.

2. Ask those who are his/her friends to come and join him/her.

3. The volunteer is to position these friends according to the rules (given below).

4. When the volunteer has positioned the friends, ask all the group to note their positions.

**5.** Then ask each of the friends in turn if they would like to move or to move anyone.

**6.** When all the friends have done this, ask the group (who are watching) to reposition the friends in the way it appears to them from outside the friendship. (This can be far more honest than the friends often are.)

**7.** When this is done, review the major differences, e.g. was X positioned by Y, but over there by Z? Let people share how they felt as well as what happened.

## RULES

**1.** The closer your friendship with people, the nearer they should stand to you.

**2.** The more of your attention they have, the more in front of you they should be; and the less of your attention they have, the further behind they should be.

**3.** The more you look up to them, the taller they should be made (stand them on a chair). The more you look down on them, the smaller they should be.

**4.** The more of their attention you think you have, the more they should face towards you; and the less of their attention you think you have, the less they should face towards you.

# HINTS

This method could be used to look at how we feel or felt

- as a child
- in class
- at home
- in this group
- at school.

Handle this carefully, as people may have emotional hurts in these areas.

You could ask someone to arrange the rest of the group to show how people are perceived spiritually:

- Height – more spiritual/less spiritual.
- Facing – more time with God facing one way; less time with God facing the other way.
- Closer – more important.
- Further away – less important.

# TALK-TO

Talk about how things are not always what they seem, e.g. some people may look holy but really are not (Jesus talking about the Pharisee and the tax collector); or how we need to be open and honest about our faith. Close in prayer.

# Honest Truth

## AIM

To enable the group to be honest about each other when describing each other's good and bad points, and to increase group awareness.

## EQUIPMENT

A set of cards as listed below, but alter them to fit the particular needs of your group. Use sheets of A4 paper cut into eight pieces.

## PREPARATION

Write out the cards.

## MAIN ACTIVITY

1.  Everyone is seated in a circle and the cards are placed face down in the middle.

2.  Choose a person (A) to draw the first card. That person reads it silently and then gives it to the person whom it best describes (B).

3.  B can choose whether or not to read out to the rest of the group the card he or she has been given.

4. B then takes a card from the middle and reads it silently. B then passes it to the person whom it best describes.

5. This continues until all the cards have been used. Some people will have lots of cards, some will have a few and some perhaps none at all.

## DEBRIEF

1. All the group read their cards in turn, prefixing each statement with 'I am ...' if they agree, or 'Someone thinks that I am ...' if they disagree.

2. At the end, each person has the opportunity to give one of their own cards to someone in the group whom they feel it more accurately describes.

3. Each person can also take one card from someone else if they wish, to add it to their own set of cards.

4. Ask the group at this stage: Who is happy with their cards and who is not?

5. Each person in turn may take another card from anyone's pile and give it to someone else.

6. When the group have completed this, ask again: Who is happy with their cards and who is not?

7. Everyone then reads their cards again, saying 'I am ...' or 'The group feels that I am ...'

**8.** Talk to the group, ensuring that they feel affirmed and 'built up' rather than 'knocked down'. Assure them of their acceptance by God and end with prayer.

## HINTS

This exercise can produce a strong emotional response. This may initially be on a superficial level, but as the task progresses do not be surprised if there is a marked change in your young people as they begin to realize how other people see them. Sometimes there are tears, at other times there is lots of laughter, but there is always increased openness and a growing together. Be prepared, though, to talk, pray and spend time with people afterwards. Also, ensure that your behaviour towards the group always reinforces God's acceptance of them.

132

## CARDS

The easiest person to talk to.
The girl who talks to the boys the most.
The person who thinks the most about others.
The person who is the most generous.
The most dominant person.
The person who makes me feel the most frustrated.
The most sensitive person.
The most forgiving person.
The person furthest from Christ.
The most honest person.
The person with the nicest eyes.
The person with the nicest hair.
The person with the most kissable lips.
[Add about 25 more.]

# Video News Reports

## AIM

To develop teamwork, decision-making and prioritizing skills within the group.

## PREPARATION

Borrow or hire a video camera and prepare the news items, either using the example given below or preparing some of your own. You will need an identical set of news items for each team.

## MAIN ACTIVITY

**1.** Split the group into two or more equal-sized teams, depending on the size of your group. Give each team a Task Card as below:

---

### News Team Task Card

Your task as the news team is to produce a five-minute news broadcast for everyone within a three-mile radius of the church.

The news will be broadcast after precisely one hour, when a video camera will be brought into the newsroom for six minutes to record the five-minute broadcast.

---

2.  Over a period of one hour, give each news team the same pieces of 'news' at odd intervals. News should arrive throughout the hour, even during the last few minutes.

3.  Record the news stories as outlined in the Task Card. The extra minute allows for the news team to cut to journalists in the field, sports reporters, the weather presenter etc.

4.  Bring the news teams together to watch their news broadcasts.

## TALK-TO

1.  Ask the groups how they feel they coped in the following areas:

    - Communication, leadership, teamwork.
    - Presentation, style, order, rambling, timing.
    - Bias, accuracy.
    - Decision-making, deciding what is newsworthy and what is not.

2.  This activity gives rise to a number of issues that would be worth discussing further.

### News Stories

*National train strike*

Many commuters stayed at home. Roads crowded. No trains will be running. Local union spokesperson said, 'Industrial action will be repeated if no solution can be found.' Local MP called on both sides to go to the arbitration service ACAS.

## Prince Charles to visit

The visit has been planned for the opening of the new hospice. Fund-raising chairman for the new 23-bed hospice says, 'We are delighted'. Local primary-school heads said children would have the afternoon off to see the Prince.

## Planning permission

Last night's Borough Council Planning Committee meeting approved the controversial Sickle Mill Flats, to be built on one of the few remaining green areas in the town. The flats, which will cost over £200,000 each, are intended for young executives. Local opposition councillors called the plan disgraceful and urged the Chairman of the Planning Committee to resign.

## Police warning

Off licences and pubs are warned in a letter from the Chief Constable that the police are clamping down on under-age drinking, following the tragic death of a 15-year-old due to the effects of excess alcohol.

## Latest news

A fire at the museum last night caused over £5,000 worth of damage. The Fire Brigade are still at the scene. Local people helped to rescue many treasures, including the famous fifteenth-century map of the town.

## Robbery

Smith & Woodward's electrical shop on East Street was broken into over the weekend. Back window smashed. Thief got away with two portable CD players.

## Robbery Update

A local youth is helping police with their enquiries. A police spokesman said, 'An arrest is expected shortly.'

## Water shortage

The local Water Authority announced a ban on the use of hosepipes and urged consumers to reduce consumption following the hottest and driest May and June on record. Reservoir levels were described as a cause for concern.

## Roadworks

Major disruption continues for road users. Gas-pipe laying has now moved into Church Road, and traffic is being diverted via Junction Place. A Gas Board official has said that the work will last for another two weeks.

## Swimming pool summer opening

After last month's opening of the new learner pool at Hamblemere Swimming Baths, the Manager announced that the pool would be open from 10 a.m. to 12 noon and from 2 p.m. to 4 p.m. every day throughout the summer holidays.

## Unrest in China

Student protests continued in many parts of China. The authorities have made hundreds of arrests. No official information from the Chinese government.

## Accident

Police are seeking witnesses to a hit-and-run accident. The accident occured at 6.45 p.m. on Chase Lane, when a red Escort crashed into the side of Fiona Jones' VW Polo, causing extensive damage.

## Kittens rescued

Six kittens were rescued from a council tip today when a workman heard their faint cries. The kittens, although dehydrated, are now doing well.

## Fire update

The fire at the museum caused £50,000 worth of damage and not £5,000, as originally broadcast.

## Church fete

Local church fete raises over £4,000 for missionary work in Nepal. Revd Timothy Fletcher was delighted by local people's support of overseas mission.

## Weather

Hot weather to continue. Maximum today 19 degrees. Minimum tonight 11 degrees. Long-range forecast: dry and hot.

## Sport

England at 240 for 3 on the first day of the second Test. Local athlete selected for England in international match against Germany.

# Collages of God

## EQUIPMENT

Magazines, PVA glue, large sheets of sugar paper, bits of crepe paper, tissue, newspapers etc. (but no scissors).

## MAIN ACTIVITY

1. Start with an introductory talk-to along these lines: 'When we talk about God we all have different ideas of what he is like. [Give appropriate examples for your group, e.g. some may see him as a policeman, judge, clown, father ...] We are going to try to put down on paper something of how we see God. Using the magazines and other materials, we are each going to assemble a collage of God.'

2. Give them plenty of time to complete this.

3. When everyone has finished, gather the group together and ask them, one at a time, to explain their collage before sticking it up on the wall.

4. When everyone has shared about their picture, move into a concluding talk-to like this: 'We all have different ideas of what God is like, but what matters is the truth about his nature. Philip, one of Jesus' disciples, asked Jesus what God was like. [Read John

14:8–11.] So if we want to know what God is
like we need to look at Jesus.'

## GOING FURTHER

1. A Bible study on Jesus – his life, teaching,
   ministry etc. Or

2. Pray that the Holy Spirit will guide all of you
   into all truth as you look at Jesus' life over the
   coming weeks.

# Creating Me

## EQUIPMENT

Clay, plastic sheeting.

## PREPARATION

Cover your tables with plastic sheeting if they will be ruined by the clay. Divide the clay into fairly large chunks (one per person).

## MAIN ACTIVITY

1. Give everyone a chunk of clay. Tell them that they are meant to use it to make an animal that is like themselves. It can be a real animal, present or extinct – e.g. a tiger or a dinosaur; or it could be an imaginary animal.

2. When they have all finished their animals (this may or may not include painting etc.), gather the group together. If the group is large you may need to divide into sub-groups. Ask them in turn to show their animal to the group and talk about how it is like them (leaders should take part in this too).

3. After everyone has shared, have a feedback time, either orally or in writing, when people can make comments or ask questions about other people's animals.

**4.** Finish with animal biscuits and drinks.

# GOING FURTHER

This is a great introduction for a short talk on a number of different subjects, such as:

**1.** We are made in the image of God, the characteristics that separate people from animals; what the Bible says; how we live out the reality of being made in the image of God.

**2.** Everyone is different; we all have different gifts, both natural and spiritual; different does not mean better or worse; all gifts are needed for the Church to fulfil Christ's commission.

# Masks

## EQUIPMENT

Paper bags, string, paint, paper, newspaper, glue, cardboard boxes, chicken wire, scissors, balloons.

## MAIN ACTIVITY

1. Everyone makes themselves a mask for a situation of their choice (e.g. home, school, with friends). The masks can be made in the following ways:

   - *Paper-bag masks.* Large paper bags, or paper carrier bags. Stick bits on, paint, cut out holes etc. as appropriate.
   - *Balloon masks.* Blow up a balloon, tie a knot, then coat one side of it in layers of papier-mâché (newspaper soaked in wallpaper paste). Then build up nose, chin, mouth shapes etc. When dry, cut out eyes and mouth, paint, stick on string hair etc.
   - *Papier-mâché and wire masks.* Using the chicken wire as a frame, build up the layers of papier-mâché. Allow to dry, then paint etc. as for balloon masks. These masks are stronger.
   - *Cardboard-box masks.* One or more cardboard boxes can be cut up and stuck together using tape and glue. Then paint and decorate the boxes. These are good

for animal masks, as it is easier to add ears and noses etc.

2. When everyone has made their mask, or while they are drying, divide into groups and give them the questionnaire. When they have completed it get feedback from all the groups.

---

### Questionnaire

1. What masks do your friends wear?

2. What masks do you wear
   (a) at school?
   (b) at church?
   (c) at home?
   (d) with friends?

3. What stops you being yourself in these different situations?

4. How does God see you?

---

## TALK-TO

1. God sees you as you are. You can hide (like Adam in the garden) or run away, but God knows you.

2. God loves you as you are and accepts you as you are. You don't have to be someone different for God to love you.

3. God wants you to be real and to get rid of your masks and begin a new life with him.

# HINTS

Papier-mâché can take a long time to dry, so you may have to do this activity over two weeks, or replace papier-mâché with Mod-roc, which dries more quickly.

# Emotions on Paper

## EQUIPMENT

Large sheets of coloured sugar-paper, paints, brushes, water.

## PREPARATION

Lay out the tables, paints, paper etc.

## MAIN ACTIVITY

1. Brainstorm a list of emotions onto a flipchart or overhead projector.

2. Ask the group members to choose an emotion that represents how they feel.

3. Everyone chooses a large piece of paper of appropriate colour and paints a picture that represents the emotion or mix of emotions that he or she can identify with.

4. Give them plenty of time to plan and produce their pictures. When they've finished lay the pictures out on the floor.

5. Assemble the group and ask people to explain their picture.

# TALK-TO

Say something along these lines: 'Some people say it is bad to show emotion, but God created us with emotions, and all that God created is good. Hiding or burying our emotions is harmful. Jesus had emotions like us.'

*Either* get the group to look up the Bible passages below to discover the emotions felt by Jesus; *or* run through the passages yourself, pointing out the emotions.

1. Matthew 21:12–13    Righteous anger
2  Matthew 20:34       Compassion
3.  Luke 13:34         Sorrow
4.  Mark 14:33         Distressed
5.  Mark 10:21         Love
6.  John 4:6           Tiredness
7.  John 11:35         Wept
8.  John 13:21         Troubled in spirit

Finish with some comments like this: 'Because Jesus knows what it is like to feel betrayed, tired, lonely etc., he can understand our prayers when we turn to him, and it is when we are open to his Spirit that he can heal our emotional scars.'

# The Armour of God

## EQUIPMENT

Newspaper, sticky tape, paper, pens.

## ACTIVITY

1. Read Ephesians 6:10–18 to the group and put the following list up on a flipchart:

   **The armour of God**
   - Belt of Truth
   - Breastplate of Righteousness
   - Gospel Shoes
   - Shield of Faith
   - Helmet of Salvation
   - Sword of the Spirit

2. Divide the group into pairs (if there is an uneven number, put a leader with the one left over).

3. Each pair chooses a champion to be dressed in the armour of God, and a dresser.

4. Each pair is given a reel of sticky tape, the newspapers are put in a pile on the floor, and the dressers are told that they have to dress their champion in the armour of God.

5. After about 20 minutes, judge the best armour.

**6.** Divide the group into six sub-groups. Give them each a part of the armour and ask them to write down the characteristics of their part.

**7.** Report back as a whole group.

# Edible Collages

Collages are great fun and young people love making them. But what do you do with them when the evening is over, especially if the young people don't want to take them home? After many years of storing them in the youth group cupboard and having an annual clear-out, we came up with the ultimate solution: let the young people eat them!

## INGREDIENTS

To prevent a drastic drop in numbers the following week, edible collages require slightly different ingredients from normal ones.

Two decisions to make: is your collage going to be sweet or savoury, and is it going to be two- or three-dimensional?

For a basic two-dimensional edible collage you will need: rice paper, sugar glue (dissolve as much sugar as you can in half a litre of water, heat it, then allow it to cool), coloured sherbet, food colouring, paint-brushes (clean and sterile), icing sugar and coloured sugars.

For a more three-dimensional collage add other ingredients – icing, sweets, cake decorations, marzipan etc. – but they will need to be displayed flat.

# IDEAS FOR COLLAGES

1. Make a collage of your moods: your opinion of yourself, how others see you etc. Use this as an opportunity for sharing about oneself.

2. Collages of how God sees you.

3. Collages of how we see God – what his character is like etc.

4. Collages of a Bible scene or an incident in Jesus' life.

# Banner Making

Banners are a great way of decorating the youth group meeting-place, and they can be made cheaply and easily.

## HOW TO DO IT

1.  Draw or find a design that you would like on the banner and photocopy it. If it is over-complicated trace out the basic design in black. When you have the required design, copy it on to an acetate sheet.

2.  Take the sheet/piece of material etc. that you are making the banner on and pin it to a wall. With an OHP project the image onto the sheet.

3.  Draw round the outline in charcoal.

4.  Take the banner down from the wall and place it on a plastic sheet to paint it. (Newspaper tends to stick, whereas a plastic sheet peels easily away and can be used many times.)

5.  Paint the design on. Emulsion paint is the cheapest and easiest, but other kinds of paint tend to have better colours.

6.  When the banner has been painted, carefully peel it off the plastic sheet (this is a two-person job) and hang it up to dry, making sure

that it is not in contact with anything. You may need to put a clothes line up in the hall to peg it to.

**7.** After it has dried you can rivet the corners so that it can be tied to a pole and hung.

## Under Construction

### AIM

To look at the cultural gap between the Church and young people and to find ways of crossing it.

### WARM-UP

Play some appropriate ice-breakers.

### EQUIPMENT

Newspapers, sticky tape, cotton reels, cocktail sticks, a set of kitchen weights.

### PREPARATION

Draw up some Instruction Cards (see below).

### MAIN ACTIVITY

1. Divide the group into two equal teams of between three and five young people.

2. Each team is given a cotton reel, sticky tape, a pile of newspapers, some cocktail sticks and an Instruction Card.

3. The teams have 10 minutes to plan and 20 minutes to build a bridge.

4. When they have finished, the leader measures the length of the bridge and applies the weights until the bridge breaks. Points are calculated and the winning team is announced.

## TALK-TO

1. 'Today we are looking at bridge building between the world of young people and the world of the Church. What are the characteristics of both?'

2. Brainstorm the characteristics onto two long pieces of paper, then put them on the wall several metres apart.

3. Give everyone a small piece of paper and ask them to write down ways of bridging the gap. Use these to build a 'bridge of suggestions' on the wall.

4. Ask the young people to choose the two (or more) best ideas. Each team takes one idea and plans how to put it into action.

5. Put it into action and see what happens.

## Fruit Dragsters

## AIM

A fun introduction to a look at the fruit of the Spirit.

## PREPARATION

A variety of fruits (some of them should be unusual ones), cocktail sticks, cutting and peeling equipment, a board or plank (set up on a slope) to run the dragsters down.

## MAIN ACTIVITY

**1.** Divide the group into teams of two to four. Each team has to design and build a fruit dragster that looks fantastic and also goes like a rocket. This is an opportunity for the kids to really use their imaginations.

**2.** The dragsters will be judged on how they look, how far they travel (after being released to roll down the slope) and their top speed.

**3.** When all the groups have made their dragsters, have a judging session on how they look. Then allow each dragster two runs down the board. Use the longest run for the distance and estimate the speeds (fast, OK, slow etc). When all the competitors have raced, the judges announce the winners and award an appropriate prize. The losers have to eat their dragsters!

## GOING FURTHER

1. Ask the groups to decide which is the most important for the Christian life: how we look, or what our top speed is, or how far we get.

2. While the groups are talking about this, give a Bible to each person/group and look at Galatians 5:22–24.

3. For each characteristic of the Holy Spirit (i.e. love, joy, peace etc.) the groups have to decide what it affects most – how we look, or how far we get, or the speed we move at in our Christian lives.

4. Ask the groups to share their answers, taking one characteristic at a time.

## TALK-TO

'It matters how we look as Christians because it should reflect the reality of what God is doing on the inside.

'It matters how fast we go. God calls us to follow him, to change, to move on where he is leading.

'It matters how far we go. Too many young people drop out of the Christian faith long before they reach the finishing line. We need to do more than roll down the slope. We need to be powered up by God himself.'

Close with a prayer of commitment or rededication.

## Glass Painting

## AIM

Using glass paints to prepare candle-jars for worship. For a winter evening.

## PREPARATION

Collect some old jars big enough to contain a lighted candle, and/or purchase some small sheets of glass. Buy a selection of glass paints and brushes. Write each of the following Bible references onto a card:

Luke 11:33–36      Psalm 27:1–3
John 1:1–9         Ephesians 5:8–11
John 8:12          1 John 1:5–7

## MAIN ACTIVITY

1. Each person decorates their jar with patterns, words, colours and symbols that say something about the gifts, experiences and understanding of God they bring to the group or to worship. It can be helpful to give out the small sheets of glass for the young people to practise painting on glass.

2. When they have finished and the paint is drying, divide the group into pairs. Tell them to take one of the Bible-verse cards and to think about what God is saying about light in this

passage, and how they can apply that as a group and as individuals. When a pair have done this, they can return the card and take another.

**3.** Gather the group back together to share their thoughts about the Bible passages.

## LATER

When the paint has dried, use the jars with lighted candles in a worship or prayer time, either to light the room or in a gathering ritual where all the jars are laid out as a Cross. Group members light the candle in their jar at the start of the worship to visibly show that they are gathered round the Cross. Or 'We meet in Jesus' Light' etc.

## ALTERNATIVES

Instead of using the candle-jars in a group time, individuals could paint mission needs on the jars (i.e. people, places, countries etc.), and members of the group could find a time each week to light the candle and pray for that mission need.

# Pizzas of Faith

## AIM

To encourage the young people to talk about their faith journey and where they are at now.

## PREPARATION

Gather together everything needed to make home-made pizzas. Depending on the time available, the group could make their own bases; if time is short, use ready-prepared or pre-packed bases. As well as the usual cheese, ham or pineapple toppings, have some more unusual ones – e.g. beans, chocolate sauce etc.

## ACTIVITY

1.  Each person is to make a pizza that represents one or more of the three situations below:

    • A high point in your spiritual journey.
    • A low point in your spiritual journey.
    • Where you are now in your spiritual journey.

2.  When everyone has designed and made their pizzas, cook them. While they are cooking,

*Either*
- Have a quiet worship time.
- Play some opening-up ice-breakers.
- Tidy up and wash up.
- Have a short Bible study on spiritual ups and downs.
- Do the notices.
- Plan a future event.

*Or*
- Watch the pizzas cook!

**3.** When the pizzas are ready, everyone in turn shares with the whole group what the meaning of their pizza is. Then eat them!

**4.** Alternatively, play this pizza-sharing game:
- Everyone cuts their pizza into four, six or eight pieces, depending on time, pizza size and group size.
- No one can eat a piece of their own pizza.
- Person A asks another member of the group (Person B) to tell them about their pizza's meaning.
- If A thinks B has given a detailed enough explanation, then A gives B a piece of A's pizza.
- Each person can only share once with the same person.
- Carry on until all the pizza is eaten.

**5.** After the pizza is eaten, spend some time talking about the ups and downs of the spiritual journey. (Use ideas from the short Bible study if you choose that option.) Finish by praying together.

# Jesus the Only Way

## AIM

To demonstrate the biblical teaching that Jesus is the only way to the Father.

## PREPARATION AND EQUIPMENT

Bibles, an Ordnance Survey map (1:50,000 scale), cards with Bible verses on. Make several photocopies of the map, with instructions.

## WARM-UP

Divide the group up into teams of four or five members, and choose one of the warm-ups below.

### Sincerely!

Each team nominates a couple to come to the front in turn and role-play one of the pair proposing to the other. The other teams give marks for believability and sincerity. In order for this to work, it needs to be fast and spontaneous.

# DIY tasks

This warm-up is a team game based on accumulated individual times to complete various tasks. The first person from each team is given a task, e.g. changing a plug. They can all do the task at the same time, but each person has to complete the task against the clock. After they have finished and the times have been recorded, the second member of each team comes out and is given a different task (see table below):

|          | Team 1               | Team 2               | Team 3               | Team 4               |
|----------|----------------------|----------------------|----------------------|----------------------|
| Person 1 | Change plug          | Insert screw         | Change tap washer    | Chisel brick in half |
| Person 2 | Chisel brick in half | Change plug          | Insert screw         | Change tap washer    |
| Person 3 | Change tap washer    | Chisel brick in half | Change plug          | Insert screw         |
| Person 4 | Insert screw         | Change tap washer    | Chisel brick in half | Change plug          |

Total all the time points at the end to see who the winner is. (The winner is the team with the smallest total time score at the end of the game.) If any tasks are not completed, agree on a standard time to award (e.g. 10 minutes ... an hour!).

# Journeys

Give each team an identical photocopy of a portion of the Ordnance Survey Map, complete with instructions and grid references.

The aim of the exercise is to plan the route of a walk from 'X' to 'Y' as marked on the map. Each team should be given the same route to plan, as if they were really going to walk the route, taking into consideration stops and camping facilities, as the whole distance would be too far to be walked in one day. Tailor the route and considerations according to the abilities and knowledge of your group, and give them help where necessary.

Ask the teams to report back on the routes they have chosen and why.

## MAIN ACTIVITY

1.  Is Jesus to be seen as a route from 'X' to 'Y' and just one route among many possible routes? Christianity has always taught that Jesus is the only way.

2.  Prepare a set of six Bible-verse cards for each team. Each card should have one of the verses listed below. All the teams should have the same six verses. To avoid confusion, each team's cards should be a different colour.

3.  One person from each team comes and collects the first Bible-verse cards. They have to take it back to their team, look it up in the Bible and decide, from the verse, how we get to heaven. They write down the answer and then come up for the second verse, and so on until all the teams have finished. Spend a short time sharing some of the discoveries.

    The verses are:

    John 14:6  Ephesians 2:8–9  1 Timothy 1:15
    Acts 2:21  Romans 10:13    1 Peter 3:21

## CONCLUSION

Draw the session together using the following to link in the Bible discoveries and any of the warm-ups used at the beginning.

1. Sincerity is not the issue. Salvation is only found through Jesus. Many of the other religions do not even have salvation as something that is offered in any real sense.

2. DIY: Doing good things, striving to be a good person and being 'religious' is not the issue either. We cannot earn a place in heaven, as some religions teach. Eternity in heaven is a free gift.

3. Salvation is found only through Jesus, and because of this there really cannot be much point in following any other path.

# Christmas

## PREPARATION

From newspapers and magazines collect some pictures of famous people – e.g. TV personalities, pop stars, film stars, sports-people, politicians. Mount them individually on cards. You will need between 10 and 20 of them, depending on the size of your group.

## OPENER

Name the personalities.

## STAGE 1

**1.** Brainstorm all the things that members of the group can remember about the Christmas story, and write them all up onto separate cards (e.g. Jesus was born in Bethlehem; Jesus, Mary and Joseph fled to Egypt; the shepherds were visited by angels etc.).

**2.** When the group have done this, ask them to put all the cards into chronological order. Then ask them to tell the story as they have made it.

## STAGE 2

**1.** Divide the group into three teams and give each team some Bibles.

- One team is to look at John's Gospel and Mark's Gospel.
- One team is to look at Matthew's Gospel.
- One team is to look at Luke's Gospel.

**2.** Each team has to read carefully the relevant part of the Gospel(s) that they have been given and find out what is said about Jesus' birth. Whenever they find something that they have already written on a card they are to tick the card.

**3.** When each team has finished, eliminate all the cards that have not been ticked, and re-read the events as they now stand.

## DISCUSS

**1.** What events did we eliminate? What did we forget and miss?

**2.** Were the group surprised to find out what the Bible does not say?

**3.** Do we get distracted from what Christmas is really about by all the 'add-ons'?

**4.** How would the group explain Christmas in one sentence to a non-Christian friend, without any jargon?

## JUST FOR FUN

**1.** Collect some pictures of famous personalities, and put them up on the walls around the room.

2. Ask the group to imagine that they are putting on a 'modern' nativity play, and the people around the room are the potential cast.

3. Who would be cast in which roles? Allow one extra personality in addition to those you have chosen.

4. Share and enjoy the cast lists and the explanations!

## Overcomplicating Christianity

### AIM

To investigate what the Christian Gospel is.

### EQUIPMENT

Paper, pencils, postage-stamp-sized pieces of paper, Bibles, questionnaires.

### PREPARATION

Photocopy the GNIKOOL Questionnaire (see overleaf).

### WARM UP

Give everyone a copy of the GNIKOOL Questionnaire. Give them 10 minutes to complete it. Share answers. (N.B. Each box on the sheet represents a word or sentence in a coded form. E.g. for number 20 the answer is 'Looking backwards'.)

# The GNIKOOL Questionnaire

| 1 | 2 | 3 | 4 |
|---|---|---|---|
| N<br>W<br>O<br>T | SAND | PROGRAMME | PUT<br>KILOGRAM |
| **5**<br><br>CHEEKKEEHC | **6** ANOTHER<br>ANOTHER<br>‖‖‖ ANOTHER<br>ANOTHER<br>ANOTHER<br>ANOTHER | **7**<br><u>KNEE</u><br>LIGHTS | **8**<br><u>MAN</u><br>BOARD |
| **9**<br>W<br>I<br>N<br>D | **10**<br><u>　　　</u><br>BSc<br>PhD<br>MSc | **11**<br>R<br>O<br>ROADS<br>D<br>S | **12**<br>OHONLEE |
| **13**<br>GROUND<br><br>FEET<br>FEET<br>FEET<br>FEET<br>FEET<br>FEET | **14** CHAIR | **15**<br>ON<br>LAP LAP LAP | **16**<br>N<br>I<br>P |
| **17**<br>⊤ R A<br>WORLD<br>L ∨<br>E | **18**<br>BELT<br>HITTING | **19**<br>J<br>U<br>YOU AND ME<br>S<br>T | **20**<br>GNIKOOL |

## Answers

1 ............ 2 ............ 3 ............ 4 ............
5 ............ 6 ............ 7 ............ 8 ............
9 ............10 ............11 ............12 ............
13 ............14 ............15 ............16 ............
17 ............18 ............19 ............20 ............

## Quiz answers

1. Up town.
2. Sand box.
3. Space programme.
4. Put on weight.
5. Cheek to cheek.
6. Six of one and half a dozen of the other.
7. Neon lights.
8. Man overboard.
9. Downwind.
10. Three degrees under.
11. Crossroads.
12. Hole in one.
13. Six feet underground.
14. High chair.
15. On the last lap.
16. Pin up.
17. Travel around the world.
18. Hitting below the belt.
19. Just between you and me.
20. Looking backwards.

## TALK-TO

Some people think that Christianity is like the quiz: rather complex and full of tricks. Today we are looking at what Christianity really is.

## MAIN ACTIVITY

**1.** Ask the group to write on the stamp-sized pieces of paper what the Christian Gospel really is. Allow them about five minutes to do this, then gather them back and let them share what they wrote.

**2.** Pass out the Bibles and list the following verses where everyone can see them:

John 1:12          Acts 4:12
John 3:16–18       Romans 3:23–24
Acts 13:38

**3.** In pairs, the group should look up the verses. Then, using the verses and their first stamp-sized Gospels, they have to answer the question, 'What is the Christian Gospel?' in few enough words to fit on a stamp.

**4.** When all the pairs have done this, ask them again to share their Gospels with the group.

## TALK-TO

'It is possible to have all sorts of strange ideas of what Christianity is all about, but the Bible tells us which of these is right and wrong. If we imagine our Christian life as a journey, then the Bible is our map and guide-book and the Holy Spirit is our guide.' Close with prayer.

# The Fruit of the Spirit

## AIM

To learn about the fruit of the Spirit.

## EQUIPMENT

Fruit-juice cocktail containing as wide a variety of juices as you can find. Paper, pencils, fruit score cards, Bibles, paper cups.

## PREPARATION

Mix the fruit cocktail. Photocopy the fruit score cards.

## WARM-UP

Play some energetic ice-breaker games.

## MAIN ACTIVITY

1. Give everyone a cup of the fruit cocktail and ask them to write on their pieces of paper the ingredients they can taste.

2. Read out the ingredients and find out how many recognized each one. Were there any ingredients they could taste that were not in the cocktail?

**3.** *Talk to:* 'The fruit of the Spirit can be compared to the fruit cocktail. There is one fruit but it has many flavours. Who knows what they are?

List these on a flipchart, OHP or paper. If the group do not know, help them out with the last few. Then read Galatians 5:16–26.

**4.** Hand out a fruit score card to each person.

**5.** For each of the characteristics, ask members to give themselves a score out of 10, and then give the group a score.

**6.** In groups of three or four, share these answers and encourage comment on how people see themselves and how they see the group.

| Fruit score card | | |
|---|---|---|
| | *Me* | *Group* |
| Love<br>Joy<br>Kindness<br>Patience<br>Self-control<br>Peace<br>Goodness<br>Gentleness<br>Faithfulness | | |

# DISCUSSION

1. Were there any areas where the group scored very low? Why do you think this is?

2. Were there any areas where people as individuals scored very low? Why did you think this is?

3. Did any individuals have a personal score that the members of the small group disagreed with?

# TALK-TO

'The fruit of the Spirit is not like the gifts of the Spirit. With the gifts, we as Christians may have one but perhaps not another. But all the different flavours of fruit should be showing through in our daily lives. The fruit of the Spirit is the product of the Holy Spirit working in our lives, and so if we are not producing fruit, then maybe we are not letting the Holy Spirit work in certain areas. If you put a black sheet on an area of your lawn at home, the grass will grow yellow and die. Similarly, if areas of our lives are cut off from the Spirit, we need to repent of our sins and offer ourselves to the Holy Spirit. Then the fruit will grow.'

Close with a time of confession and a time of asking the Holy Spirit to fill everyone to overflowing.

180

# Ice Cream Evangelism

## AIM

To look at the opportunities and the problems of personal evangelism. The activity can also be used as a discussion starter on the uniqueness of Christ.

## PREPARATION

Write some one-minute topic cards.

## EQUIPMENT

Bibles, paper, pens, dice, a large sheet of paper, one-minute topic cards and a marker pen.

## WARM-UP

1.  Everyone sits in a circle.

2.  Each person rolls the dice in turn. If a 6 is thrown, that person must take a one-minute topic card and talk on that topic for one minute. If a number between 1 and 5 is thrown, the dice is simply passed on to the next person.

3.  Keep the one-minute topic cards face down so that nobody knows what they say before they are chosen.

## Topic cards

1. My pet elephant
2. School dinners
3. Sunday lunch
4. Jesus
5. Church

6. Warfare
7. Vegetarians
8. My best day
9. Blue
10. Radio

## MAIN ACTIVITY

1. Ask each person to decide what their favourite ice cream flavour is and then to get into groups with people of the same taste in ice cream. Ask the groups to say what their flavour is and the number in their group. Record this on a large displayed sheet of paper.

2. Explain now that their task is to persuade everyone else that their group's flavour is the best to be had in ice cream and to try to get them to join their group. Give them three minutes for this.

3. Now ask everyone to regather into their new groups and find the new numbers in each group. Put the figures on to the large sheet of paper. There is likely to be very little change.

4. Tell the groups that they have two minutes in which to plan a strategy by which folk from other groups might be persuaded to join their particular group. Give them two minutes.

5. Meanwhile, pick out one member from the whole group (pick two people if the group is greater than 14). Take him or her aside and explain that they have just discovered that ice

182

cream is a slow and deadly poison leading to inevitable death. Their task is to persuade people not to eat it. Introduce this person and give him or her a further three minutes to try to persuade people not to eat ice cream.

6. When the time is up, write down the final figures on the record sheet.

## DEBRIEF

- How many people changed sides?
- Why did people swap?
- Why did people stay?
- How many people responded to the poison warning?
- Why did some people not respond?
- Are there any similarities between Christianity and ice cream evangelism?

You may want to draw out these parallels:

1. All religions lead to death; Jesus is the only way to the Father (John 14:16).

2. Not many people are persuaded by argument to swap sides. Is this true when talking to people about Christianity?

3. If people were forced into other groups, did they return to their original groups soon afterwards? Is this like non-Christians who are made to attend church?

## GOING FURTHER

Divide the group into small groups of four and give them paper and pencils. Ask each group

to look at evangelism in the New Testament
using the verses given below. From this information, can they think of any ways to reach
out to their friends, family and neighbours?
Then ask all the groups to report back.

1 Corinthians 2:1–5
Acts 4:32–35
Matthew 28:19–20
John 14:15–17
Matthew 5:13–16

# Marathon Race

## AIM

To get the young people to identify where they see themselves in the Christian life.

## PREPARATION

'Running the Race' sheets – one for each person (see below).

## ACTIVITY

1. Talk about the Christian life as a race. Using the example of a marathon race, explain some of the different positions that people can be in.

2. Hand out the 'Running the Race' sheets.

3. Ask everyone to think about where they are in their spiritual life and to tick the appropriate box on the sheet. (They need to keep their answers secret at this stage.)

4. When everyone has done this, divide into groups of five.

5. Give them the following instructions:
   (a) Do not tell anyone which box you ticked yet.

# Running the Race

The Christian life has often been compared to a race. Paul writes in 2 Timothy 4:7, 'I have fought the good fight, I have finished the race. I have kept the faith.' In this exercise we will be thinking about where we are in our own Christian life and comparing it to a marathon. So, after thinking about where you are spiritually, tick the boxes beside the statements that best describe your position.

(a) *In the race:*
- ☐ Waiting at the start.
- ☐ Running hard at the beginning.
- ☐ Running hard well into the race.
- ☐ Chugging along at your own pace.
- ☐ Taking a breather.
- ☐ Slowing down.
- ☐ Given up.
- ☐ Taken a wrong turn and lost your way.

(b) *Spectating:*
- ☐ Always watch but never take part.
- ☐ Just passing, so take a look.
- ☐ Would like to join in but don't know how.
- ☐ Thinking about running but unsure.

(c) *Officiating:*
- ☐ A race marshal, always there but not in the race.
- ☐ The coach, giving advice, but not actually in the race.

(d) *Other:*
Please describe your position below, if different.

(b) For each of the people in the group, put a tick where you think they are in their spiritual life.

(c) Taking each person in the group in turn, everyone says where they have put that person and why. The person then says where he/she has put him/herself, and why.

(d) Do this for each member of the group.

**6.** Bring the groups back together, and
   (a) Ask if there are any comments.
   (b) Ask how many people were put in a different place by their group.
   (c) Talk about your spiritual life in terms of the different positions on your sheet, what you found helpful and how you have grown as a Christian. Invite comments from committed Christians within the group if they too want to say how they have found things.

## Construct-a-Christian

## AIM

To look at the young people's stereotypes of what a Christian is and to challenge these where necessary.

## EQUIPMENT

Wallpaper, paint, charcoal, scissors, chairs, tables, a bag of sweets, paper and pencils for everyone.

## PREPARATION

Make enough Instruction Cards so that each young person has one. Fill them in with a variety of ages and names, and using both sexes.

---

### Instruction Card

Your Christian is called.............................................

Age ............................. Sex ...............................

Draw a human outline. Cut it out and paint it according to how you see this person as a Christian – e.g. what would they wear? Would they be trendy? etc.

# WARM-UP

Ask for six volunteers to come out to the front to be your panel of experts. Sit them on the chairs in two rows of three, behind the tables. Two contestants taken from the rest of the group come out to the front to attempt to win a packet of sweets. The game is played as follows:

1. Give each contestant in turn a word.

2. The contestant and the panel members write down on the paper provided the first thing that the given word brings to mind.

3. The contestant and then the panel share what they wrote.

4. The contestant scores one point for each member of the panel who has written the same answer as he/she has.

5. Play two rounds. The winner is the contestant with the most points.

# MAIN ACTIVITY

1. Divide the group into teams of four.

2. Talk to the group along these lines: 'We all have stereotypical views of what summer holidays, old houses, school dinners etc. are like. What are our stereotypical images of what a Christian is like? What I want you to do is to construct a stereotypical Christian from the information given you on your Instruction Card.'

**3.** After the teams have had enough time to do this, get them all to introduce their Christian to the rest of the group and to talk about what they are like and why.

**4.** Hold a vote with the whole group as to which of the stereotypes/characters was the most probable. Then look at John 1:12 and talk about what a Christian is really like – i.e. someone who has received Jesus as his/her Lord and Saviour and who is a child of God.

# Heroes and Villains

## AIM

To demonstrate that in Jesus Christ we discover how God intended people to live.

## EQUIPMENT

Lots of newspaper, a tape-player etc., paper, pens.

## PREPARATION

Tape some 'hero' music and some 'villain' music (from TV, radio etc.)

## WARM UP

Find three or four extrovert members of the youth group to act out being heroes to the hero music and villains to the villain music. Get the group to decide who was the best.

## MAIN ACTIVITY

1.  Tip the newspaper into a heap in the middle of the floor.

2.  Everyone has to hunt through until they find someone in an article who they see as a hero and someone they see as a villain.

**3.** Then write the characteristics of the person they have chosen that make him or her a hero/villain.

**4.** Ask people to read out the name of their heroes and their characteristics, and state why they chose them.

**5.** Write the characteristics (but not the names of the people chosen) up on a flipchart under two headings, Positive and Negative.

**6.** *Talk-to:* 'Looking at the list on the flipchart, can we imagine someone with all the positive qualities and no negatives? Jesus was perfect – he had all the positive qualities but none of the negatives, and that is what God intended us to be like when he created us. But we rebelled and are rebelling against God still. So he sent his Son to live a perfect life. The religious people crucified him, but God raised him to life. Today we don't just have the example of Jesus' life, we can also have the power to be like him by having the Holy Spirit within us.'

**7.** Ask the group members to each write a positive and a negative characteristic of theirs on a piece of paper, and in a time of silent prayer to thank God for the positive and to ask his help with the negative.

**8.** Then close in prayer.

# Taking Your Temperature

## AIM

To assess where your group stands on a variety of moral, personal and spiritual issues.

## PREPARATION

Cut out squares of coloured card – each person needs nine cards, each of a different colour.

## EQUIPMENT

Bibles, pencils, cards cut and sorted into colours as above. Blu-tak, four pieces of paper marked 'hot', 'cold', 'pro' and 'anti'.

## WARM-UP

Play a number of warm-up ice-breakers.

## MAIN ACTIVITY

1.  Give each person nine cards (one of each colour) and ask them to put their name in large letters on one side and a piece of Blu-tak on the other.

**2.** Label one end of the room 'hot' and the other end 'cold', one side of the room 'pro' and the other side 'anti'.

**3.** Explain to the group as follows:
(a) We're going to name a number of issues, each of which has been allocated a colour.
(b) For each of the issues, take your card of the same colour and place it on the floor near the label which most closely identifies your feelings on the issue.
(c) If you feel very concerned or an issue is important to you, place your card nearer the 'hot' end of the room. If you are less concerned, place your card nearer the other end.
(d) If an issue is something you feel is 'right' or is one you strongly agree with, place your card on the side of the room marked 'pro'. But if the issue is something you feel is 'wrong' or is one you disagree with, place your card on the 'anti' side of the room.
(e) It is possible to be very 'pro' on an issue at the same time as being very 'hot'. Similarly, you may wish to place your card on the 'anti' and 'cold' section of the room.

**4.** Taking one issue at a time, ask each person to stick their corresponding coloured card, names uppermost, onto the floor in the part of the room which they feel represents their views.

**5.** When all the cards have been placed in position, let everyone have a look to see where everyone is positioned.

*Cards:*

| | |
|---|---|
| Abortion | White |
| Pre-marital sex | Red |
| Church | Yellow |
| School | Pale Blue |
| Parents | Pink |
| Jesus | Orange |
| Youth group | Dark blue |
| Environment | Light green |
| Smoking | Dark green |

**6.** Lead into a discussion. Here are some suggestions:

(a) What was the issue everyone felt most agitated about?

(b) What was the issue people felt least agitated about?

(c) What were people most pro and most anti on?

(d) What is the group most divided about?

(e) What is the group most united about?

(f) How did the Church rate when compared with Jesus? Why do you think this is?

# GOING FURTHER

Divide into four groups and give each group a card listing a subject and Bible references (see below) to investigate and then to report back on. You could deal with any number of issues. For example:

| *1. Abortion* | *2. Pre-marital sex* | *3. Parents* |
|---|---|---|
| Jeremiah 1:5 | Genesis 2:24 | Exodus 20:12 |
| Luke 1:39–45 | 1 Corinthians 6:12–20 | Ephesians 6:1–4 |

# The Gulag Gospel

## AIM

To help the teenagers understand what it is like to live under an anti-Christian régime, and also to find out how well they know their Bible.

## EQUIPMENT

Pen and paper for each group. Flipchart or overhead projector.

## PREPARATION

Get in touch with Amnesty International and ask for details of Christians who are persecuted for their faith. You may wish to ask for a particular country. Amnesty's regular magazine has a church section which reports on those Christians who have been imprisoned for their faith. It is helpful if you can talk about individual cases of persecution. Pass around photographs showing cases of harassment or victimization. In fact use anything which will make the subject more real – photos, letters, newspaper articles, slides, a video etc.

## MAIN ACTIVITY

1. When the group gets together, confiscate all Bibles. (This may not be a problem if your teenagers are not in the habit of bringing

theirs along!) Then ask them to imagine that they live in a country which is hostile to Christians and actively persecuting believers. Because of their faith they are sentenced to a labour camp, and are not allowed to take any of their personal belongings.

2.  Put everyone into small groups (pairs or fours), and provide each group with pen and paper. Tell them that they are a group of Christians in the labour camp, all Bibles and religious literature have been confiscated, and they have to see how much of the Bible they remember and write down as accurately as possible. But before they scream 'That's impossible!' ask them if they can remember some of the key events of the Gospel. Using the overhead projector or flipchart, note them down under the categories of parables, miracles, teaching, significant events.

3.  Ask each group to choose one of the suggested incidents or stories and write it down as accurately as they can remember. Give them about 10–15 minutes for this, then ask each group in turn to read out what they have written. The other groups can contribute if they wish.

4.  When each group has had its turn, see if you can arrange the events in chronological order.

## TALK-TO

There is a multitude of issues for teaching arising out of the Gulag Gospel. You could talk about the importance of the Bible, its nature and historical background, what it reveals to us of God. Also talk about the importance of the help and support that other believers can give by their knowledge of God and the Bible. You might find this session very revealing on how much both teenagers and leaders know or don't know of the Bible.

# When the Going Gets Tough

## AIM

To look at some of our fears and misconceptions when the Christian faith seems to be very hard going.

## PREPARATION

Draw up a number of road signs with explanations (see below), and position them round the room.

## WARM-UP

1. Brainstorm what the members find tough about the Christian life onto an overhead projector or flipchart. After the list has been completed, ask the group to look at the road signs you have placed round the room.

SING IT AGAIN –
EVERYTHING WILL
BE ALL RIGHT.

NO
DOUBT
ENTRY

YOU CAN'T BE
A REAL CHRISTIAN
IF YOU DOUBT.

THIS TIME YOU'VE
BLOWN IT –
NO RETURN FROM
HERE.

EVERYONE ELSE IS
DOING OK – GOING
THE OTHER WAY.

IF ONLY I HAD
MORE FAITH!

YOU CAN'T ESCAPE
PAST SINS.

**2.** When everyone has had the opportunity to look at the road signs, ask them which of the signs reminded them of their own experiences of life when things get tough. Discuss these experiences in small groups.

## WORD-UP

These are the road signs of mindless Christianity. None of them is true, but when things get tough in our faith, they can look as if they might be the obvious solutions.

Let's look at some of the things we can learn from the life of David.

## BIBLE INVESTIGATION

Divide into three groups and look at the passages and questions below:

### Group 1

Read 2 Samuel 11:1–12:23 carefully!

*Thinking about the Bible*

**1.** What were the stages in David's fall into sin?

**2.** What were the stages in his repentance and restitution?

**3.** How did God use Nathan?

## Thinking about yourself

**1.** When you find yourself slipping deeper into sin (no matter how small), are there similarities between what happens to you and what happened to David? Give examples if you can.

**2.** There was an element of punishment in the restitution. How do you feel about this attribute of God's nature – how does it influence your moral behaviour?

## Group 2

Read 1 Samuel 24. (It may be worth scanning the preceding chapters as well to see Saul's attempts on David's life and the extent of his jealousy.)

## Thinking about the Bible

**1.** Discuss round your group: Who would have taken the opportunity to kill Saul and who would have acted in the same way as David? Why?

**2.** What were the consequences for Saul of David's action?

**3.** What were the consequences for David of his action? (David became king and Saul died along with his sons in battle.)

## Thinking about ourselves

**1.** David was obedient to God when he was

tempted. What temptations tend to draw us away from obedience?

2. David's men encouraged him to kill Saul, which is what Saul would probably have done if the situation had been reversed. What is the consequence for us if we listen to others rather than to God?

3. What do we learn from all this about when the going gets tough?

## Group 3

Read 1 Samuel 17:1–54. This is a well-known story, but try to read it carefully.

### Thinking about the Bible

1. What was the Philistine strategy for undermining the people of God?

2. Why and how would David have been defeated if he had used Saul's weapons?

### Thinking about ourselves

1. David defeated Goliath because he fought with his weapons, on his territory. What can we apply from this to our own spiritual battles?

2. What are the consequences for us of spiritual defeats and victories in our own personal life?

3. What do we learn about when the going gets tough in all this?

# Agony Aunt Evening

## AIM

To understand personal problems and to consider what the Christian answers to them may be.

## WARM-UP

Divide the group into fours. Ask them to describe to other members in turn, first, the best thing that ever happened to them and, secondly, the worst thing that ever happened to them.

## PREPARATION

Over the preceding weeks collect together as many problem pages as possible from various magazines. Then make a careful selection of the type of problems which your teenagers could relate to and which you want them to consider, e.g. family relationships, boy/girl partnerships, sex, honesty, personal integrity, guilt, etc.

## MAIN ACTIVITY

1. Divide into groups. According to how your young people relate to each other, you may consider it appropriate to have groups of four, or more, or indeed to stay in one large group.

**2.** Give each group three of the problem letters. You can give each group the same letters or different ones. Do not give them the Agony Aunt's reply. Ask each group to discuss what advice they would give in answer to each problem. Allow around 15 minutes.

**3.** Bring everybody together and ask each group to read out one of their problems and the advice they would give. Then open the issue up for discussion generally. You may like to draw together the salient points and mention any distinctive Christian understanding of the problem. Then it may be appropriate to read out and discuss the answer which the Agony Aunt gave.

**4.** Go through the three problems of each group or, if time is short, take just one problem from each.

## CONCLUSION

It is helpful for teenagers to appreciate the various perspectives on their own and other people's personal problems. This activity will encourage them to talk frankly and openly about sensitive subjects. It should also be an opportunity to do some teaching on Christian ethics.

Some of the issues may strike an emotional chord, so be sensitive to provide opportunity for personal conversation with individuals when the main session is over.

# The Jesus File

## AIM

To discover how much the group knows about Jesus and to get them working together.

## EQUIPMENT

Coloured duplicator paper, pens.

## WARM-UP

A few ice-breakers.

## MAIN ACTIVITY

1. Ask each person to write down from memory, on separate pieces of paper:

   (a) One thing that Jesus taught
                              (on yellow paper).
   (b) One miracle that Jesus performed
                              (on blue paper).
   (c) One person that Jesus met
                              (on green paper).
   (d) One fact about Jesus' life
                              (on pink paper).

2. When everyone has done this to the best of their ability, form them into pairs (preferably with someone they don't know well). If you have odd numbers, pair one up with a leader.

They then have to choose the six facts about Jesus which they feel are most important and which must include at least one of each colour of paper. Collect in the discarded sheets.

3. Form the pairs into groups of 6 or 8 people and tell them that from their information (i.e. their pieces of paper) they have to build a 'Gospel' containing only 15 (for groups of 8) or 12 (for groups of 6) pieces of information, with a minimum of 2 for each colour.

4. When the groups have done this, ask a spokesperson from each group to read out what they have included and put it up on a flipchart.

5. *Talk to:* 'When the Gospel writers wrote down the teaching, miracles and information about Jesus' life, they had to choose what to include and what not to include. That is why we have some things that Jesus did in some Gospels and not in others (illustrate this from the flipchart and the Bible), whereas important things are in all the Gospels [again illustrate from the flipchart and the Bible].

'What do you think was the most important thing Jesus did? He died on the cross and was raised again from the dead. That is why the Gospel writers spend so much space on the crucifixion and resurrection.'

6. Close with an appropriate prayer.

# Loneliness

## AIM

To create an opportunity for the young people to look at the issue of loneliness and some of the biblical responses to it.

## INTRODUCTION

'Today we are thinking about loneliness. We live in a society where loneliness is an epidemic. Suidices, depression and alcohol and drug abuse are all symptoms of the isolation and aloneness which many people experience every day.'

Play *'Smells like teen spirit'* by Nirvana.

## WARM-UP

1. Where would you feel most alone?
   (a) On your own on a windswept moor miles from anywhere and with the night coming down? *or*
   (b) At a party where everyone is having a great time ... except you?

2. Ask the group to go to the right-hand side of the room if they would feel more lonely in situation (a) and to the other side if they would be more lonely in situation (b).

3. Ask everyone in the group to find a partner (from the other side of the room, as far as is possible) and to spend one minute explaining to each other why they chose either option (a) or (b). In pairs, write a definition of loneliness in 20 words (maximum) on a sheet of paper that can then be put up onto the wall.

## MAIN ACTIVITY

1. Begin by giving out a Loneliness Sheet to each person.

2. For each of the eight situations, each person gives a score ranging between 1 and 5. 1 means not feeling at all lonely and 5 means being very lonely indeed. This score is entered into the first column. The second column is a record of any situations that people can identify with as something they have already experienced.

3. After the exercise has been completed, ticks and scores are totalled and written in the 'Total' box at the bottom of the sheet. These two scores then combine to produce each person's loneliness ratio. E.g. if in the left-hand column a person scores 17 and also has 3 ticks in the right-hand column, their loneliness ratio will be 17:3. This ratio can then be produced in the form of a badge or sticker to be worn for the remainder of the session.

4. The loneliness ratio can make both members and leaders more aware of those who are suffering from loneliness and related problems. The ratios do not prove anything in themselves, as it is quite possible to cheat. In

# Loneliness

| SITUATION | Score | Tick if this has happened to you |
|---|---|---|
| 1. It is Saturday evening and you are stuck at home in front of the TV. | | |
| 2. No one sits by you at lunch time. | | |
| 3. You ring a friend for a chat and they ask you to call back tomorrow. | | |
| 4. You are at home, sick for the third day in a row and no one from work, college or school called to ask you how you are. | | |
| 5. You have been chosen for a local sports team and you try to tell your parents, but they're too busy to listen at the moment. | | |
| 6. At youth group no one notices that you are feeling down or comes over to talk to you. | | |
| 7. Your group of friends are going to a concert and haven't asked you. | | |
| 8. Everyone seems to be having a good time and you don't feel part of what is going on. | | |
| Score: 1 = not lonely  5 = very lonely | | |
| TOTAL | | |

a caring group, however, they can encourage those with pastoral gifts to befriend and talk with those who are lonely. It also brings out into the open things which we often keep hidden.

## WORD UP

Our loneliness ratio can be like our blood pressure, indicating if we are in need of looking after. In what ways could we help to bring each other's ratios down? Think of those inside the group and also those outside if you can.

Get into groups of five and produce a list of possibilities for action. Choose your top three.

## REPORT BACK

After five minutes gather the groups back together and ask each group to report their top three possibilities. Put these on an overhead projector or flipchart so that everyone can see them.

## BIBLE INVESTIGATION

In pairs look at some of the things that God has to say about being alone and loneliness. (Don't give out verses to the groups unless they are stuck.) Ask the entire group:

- Where would you start?
- What verses or passages would you give to a lonely friend?

- How should the Church care more for people who are lonely?

## WORD-UP

After 10 minutes have the pairs share with the group some of the things they have discovered and some of their thoughts.

# Moral Choices

## AIM

To look at how we make moral and personal choices and decisions as Christians.

## PREPARATION AND EQUIPMENT

You will need to draw and label shapes as shown below. Use card rather than paper. Prepare enough card copies of the Moral Triangle so that everyone can have one each. Gather enough scissors so that everyone can have a pair each. You will also need a large sheet of paper or an overhead projector and pens for the brainstorm warm-up.

## WARM-UP

Play one or both of the following warm-up games.

### God wants versus my wants

Brainstorm some of the moral choices that members expect to be faced with over the next few years. After all these have been written up on a large sheet of paper, characterize each choice by marking them with one of the following:

G = God wants      M = My wants

## 'Scruples'

Borrow a game of 'Scruples' and play it for about 20 minutes: a fun way to expose people to immediate moral choice-making.

## MAIN ACTIVITY

Pass out a pair of scissors and a copy of the Moral Triangle to everyone and explain that you are going to suggest some guidelines for making moral decisions – some that are true and some that are obviously false. Each guideline will have a letter to describe it – A to G, corresponding with the shapes you have drawn.

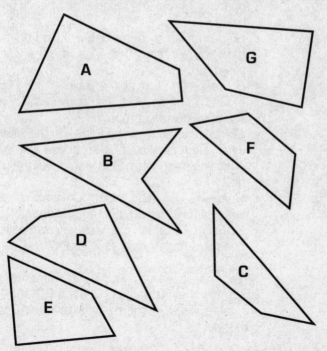

When each guideline is read out, if members think that it is a Christian way of making a decision, they are to cut out the corresponding piece of the Moral Triangle. If, at the end of the game, they have guessed correctly all the Christian guidelines, they should be able to compile an equilateral triangle from the pieces they have cut out.

## Guidelines

- *Guideline A:* Pray, asking God to guide you in your prayers.
- *Guideline B:* Look at your situation and your circumstances and see whether God is opening or closing doors for you through them.
- *Guideline C:* Lay out a deal – if God does 'x' then you will know that 'y' is what he wants you to do.
- *Guideline D:* Look at the Bible – in the light of God's call on your life, is the action you are considering compatible?
- *Guideline E:* Look at the Bible – in the light of what God is like, is the action you are contemplating what God would want you to do?
- *Guideline F:* Ask older Christians and leaders for their advice and guidance.
- *Guideline G:* Check out what you are feeling: does this feel right in your heart?

Allow members a couple of minutes to assemble their triangles. Options (C) and (G) are false ways in themselves to seek God's guidance.

## WORD-UP

Explain that feelings are very changeable as a basis for making decisions. Twisting God's arm or randomly opening our Bibles are a long way short of developing the long-lasting relationship that God is longing to have with all of us. Part of the process of building that relationship is getting to know God and discerning what his will is. Gradually we become more and more aware of what kinds of action are compatible.

## GOING FURTHER

In pairs, choose two or three of the issues that were brainstormed at the beginning of the session and that were characterized with an 'M'. Consider them in the light of Guidelines A, B, D, E and F.

# Cliques

## INTRODUCTION

Paint the picture for your group as follows: 'A youth group has decided to start two house groups so that young people may meet fortnightly on a Wednesday evening. These will be led by two of the couples who have been helping with the group on a Sunday evening. As the leader, you would like a good mixture of the committed and less committed, male and female and different ages in each group. Unfortunately, when you write a list of those who have said they are interested and add the information about the group members which you as leader have, your potential list of candidates for house groups looks something like this.'

### The candidates

*Matthew (17):* Fancies Joanne but she does not appear interested.

*Mark (15):* Has just broken up with Mary after going out with her for six months; is eyeing up Helen.

*Luke (15):* Wants 'a laugh' and would like to be in the same group as Matthew, whom he considers to be 'a laugh'.

*John (14):* Gets on well with Corinne and Phillipa: he looks up to them as being 'spiritualy mature'.

*Tim (18):* Was friends with Matthew but he is now too busy and is looking for a girlfriend.

*Corinne (18):* Wants to be in a serious Bible study group and 'do it properly'.

*Phillipa (18):* Best friends with Corinne and tries to do everything with her.

*Joanne (17):* Fancies Matthew but her parents don't want her to see him. The Minister has been told this and he has told you.

*Justine (17):* Doesn't want to be in the same group as her brother, John.

*Mary (16):* No one knows her well, as she is new.

*Rachel (15):* Fancies Tim, as does her friend Helen, and you suspect she would like to use a house group as a chance to get to know him.

*Helen (15):* Is in the same class as Luke at school and thinks he is too immature.

*Jose (15):* Hates reading out loud and is very nervous indeed about joining a group.

*Susan (14):* Doesn't want to be in a group with any of the boys because of Mark.

## TASK

In groups of four, put the candidates into two house groups which will meet the leaders' requirements and will work. The groups are then to report back as to how they have allocated the candidates.

# IN THE GROUPS

1. List your priorities for making the selections you made. What were the more important factors in your selections and what were the things that you did not take so much into account?

2. What do you feel was the members' first priority?

3. Do you think that the leaders set the right priorities?

4. In what ways is our group similar or different?

# Give It Away!

## AIM

To encourage the young people to realize that being a Christian involves sharing their faith with their friends and family.

## PREPARATION

You will need pens, paper, Bibles and a worksheet for each member of the group.

## ACTIVITY

Divide the group up into smaller groups of what you consider the optimum number for good discussion. Then hand out worksheets prepared from the ideas below.

---

### Worksheet 1

Take a look at Matthew 28:18–20 and Mark 16:15–16. What did Jesus tell us to do?

---

## Worksheet 2

Spend about 10 minutes discussing these questions with the rest of your group:

(a) Who has the nicest smile?
(b) Who has the most well-thumbed Bible?
(c) Who is the one who talks most?
(d) Who looks the most religious?
(e) Who has been a Christian the longest?
(f) Who has passed a religious education exam?
(g) Who is the most outward-going?
(h) Who became a Christian most recently?
(i) Who knows the most about God?

Now discuss this question: What are the most important qualifications for being able to tell others about God?

## Worksheet 3

Individually look at the list below and tick what you think are the three reasons why you rarely talk to others about God.

☐ I don't want others to know I'm a Christian.
☐ They would not understand.
☐ I'm not sure I know enough answers to my friends' questions.
☐ I might be persecuted for what I believe.
☐ It's not the sort of thing you talk about.
☐ My actions speak louder than words.
☐ I might be labelled a 'Bible-basher'.
☐ I'm not really that bothered.
☐ I'm not a good enough Christian.

Then discuss with your group the ones you have ticked and why you have ticked them.

## Worksheet 4

Take a look at 1 Peter 3:15–16. Discuss these questions:

(a) What does it mean by the 'hope' you have as a Christian?
(b) What are the implications of honouring Jesus as the Lord of your life?
(c) In what ways do you feel your conduct may help or indeed hinder some people in finding God?

## Worksheet 5

Finally get together in pairs and take it in turns to explain as clearly as you can what a Christian is and how you become one. Then each choose two of these verses and explain to the other what they mean: John 1:12; John 3:16; Romans 6:25; 1 Peter 2:24.

Finish by each praying for a friend you know who you think may be interested in discovering more of what it means to know God.

# Sin

## AIM

To look at the nature of sin: why does it separate us from a holy God and what has God done to make it possible to restore our relationship with him?

## WARM-UP

Choose one of the following exercises. Or you may prefer to invent a similar game to make the point.

### Ball chuck

Set up a bucket about five metres from a chair. Contestants have to stand on the chair and throw tennis balls into the bucket. The contestant keeps on throwing until a ball either misses the bucket or bounces out of it. The contestant scores the number of balls in the bucket at the end of his turn.

### Circle pull

Draw a chalk circle on the floor using a diameter of 10cm for every person playing. (For example, if there are 25 players, the circle will be 2.5m in diameter.) All players hold hands in a circle around the chalk one.

The object is to pull other players inside the chalk circle while remaining outside it yourself. Anyone treading inside the chalk circle is eliminated, and if two players let go hands in the struggle which follows, both are also out.

## MAIN ACTIVITY

**1.** Divide the group into threes. Each group of three is given a cheap, large, white T-shirt (or group members could bring their own) and marker pens.

**2.** The group write on the T-shirt every sin which they can think of in a given time limit, and then one of the group models the finished result.

**3.** Allow everyone to look at all the shirts and then have the shirt-wearers line up at the front for the whole group to vote on the 'biggest sinner'. Note the top three vote-winners.

**4.** Explain that each of the top three vote-winners has been invited to a party but it is, unfortunately, a white-shirt event and none of them is likely to get in, owing to their present state.

**5.** To help the situation, offer the shirt-wearers bottles of Tipp-Ex, or a bucket of water perhaps, to cover up their sins. To the winner of the vote you could give a bag of soap powder with a bucket of water, as a special treat!

**6.** The shirt-wearers have five minutes to make their shirt presentable for the party – let them draw on the help of the whole group if necessary. After the five minutes are up, ask them to remodel their shirts.

**7.** You can comment:

- Hold up a Tipp-Exed shirt: 'Trying to cover up our sins is really no solution; it does not solve the problem of the sins themselves, merely tries to disguise them ... badly. We are still not presentable.'
- Hold up the wet shirt: 'Trying to clean up our own act to make us presentable for the party is no help either ... we can't get rid of the stains that sin leaves.'
- Hold up the washing-powdered shirt: 'Even man-made solutions don't solve the problem completely. The problem may seem to have faded, but it is still there. Still not presentable enough for the party, I'm afraid.'
- The Bible says, 'If anyone is in Christ, they are a new creation. The old has gone ...' When God cleanses us from our sins, he doesn't cover them over, he doesn't leave the job half done and us all stained ... he makes us like a brand new shirt.'

**226**

**8.** Take all the stained shirts and put them on a large cross. Give out clean shirts to everyone.

**9.** Hold a celebration meal.

# Rejection

## AIM

To look at what happens when you are hurt by someone who rejects you and how we are to respond to this as Christians.

## EQUIPMENT AND PREPARATION

Lots of balloons, felt-tip pens.

## WARM-UPS

### Smash yer face in!

1.  Give each person a balloon and a felt pen. They should blow up their balloon, tie it and then draw a face on it to represent how they feel at that moment.

2.  When everyone has drawn the face on their balloon, go round the circle and have everyone introduce their 'face' to the rest of the group.

3.  Everyone then places their balloon on the floor in the middle of the room and goes and stands round the edge of the room.

**4.** As the command 'GO!' is given, everyone has to try to protect their 'face' without using their hands or picking it up off the floor, and at the same time try to burst other people's 'faces'.

**5.** After 30 seconds, yell 'STOP!' and see how many people are left with a 'face' still intact.

**6.** Instant share: go round the circle again and say one word which describes how you feel.

### Break in/Break out

These games are also excellent warm-ups for this session.

**1.** Divide the group into smaller groups of about six to eight members. Ask for a volunteer from each group.

**2.** The remaining group members stand in a circle around the volunteer and link arms to make a secure circle around the volunteer in the middle.

**3.** The person standing in the middle of the circle has to try to BREAK OUT! of the circle by any means possible.

**4.** BREAK IN! happens as above, but the other way round: the volunteer stands outside the circle and tries to BREAK IN! using any means possible.

**5.** After the volunteers have had a go and succeeded or failed, let others who want to have a go at either variation to experience what it feels like.

**6.** Ask the members who tried to break in or to break out:
- Which was easier: breaking in or breaking out?
- What did the experience feel like?
- What did it feel like to be excluded?
- Did anything that happened in the game make it easier or harder to cope with?

# WORD-UP

**1.** Feeling embarrassment or rejection and being trapped are some of the situations which cause us to be hurt. Here's a story about being hurt, at the end of which we are going to look at who was hurt by whom, how and why:

'Andy and Dave had been best friends for years and years. In fact they had been friends since they started secondary school. They had got on well and were now members of their local Church Youth Fellowship.

'Then it happened. Andy met Clare. She was new to church, full of life and for some reason Andy just wanted to spend loads of time with her. They didn't really do anything, just chatted and spent time together.

'One day, Dave and Andy decided to go down to the pub the following Friday evening to catch up on the news, but Andy's mind was elsewhere, especially when Clare suggested that Andy and she should spend a quiet night watching the latest video release at her place.

'On Friday night, Dave sat in the pub staring wistfully at his drink, wondering where Andy could be, and also feeling embarrassed and let down.

'The next Sunday after church, Dave had a word with Clare's best friend, Fiona, to express his worries. "Andy and Clare are seeing so much of each other: he was round there on Friday night and I'm worried that they might be sleeping together."

'Fiona was consequently worried too. She really liked Clare and didn't want to see her ruin her life and wreck her relationship with God. So, she did a Christian thing and invited four of her friends to pray for Clare after they had talked over the kinds of things that they should pray and how Clare was sleeping with Andy. They told God all the gossip.

'Next day at college, one of the friends who had been praying in the prayer group saw Clare and told her that they were all praying for her the night before so that she would have the spiritual strength to stop sleeping with Andy. Clare was furious and assumed that Andy was behind the rumour. She stormed up to him and said she never wanted to see him again.'

**2.** When you have read the story, either go over the details again or pass out photocopies of it so that everyone can read it.

**230**

**3.** Hand out a Rejection Sheet (as below) to everyone and ask them to think about the story and then fill in their sheet.

**4.** For the behaviour rank column: put a 1 next to the person who behaved the best; a 2 next to the person who behaved second best, and so on through to a mark of 5 for the person who behaved the worst. For the hurt rating:

give each person a mark out of 10 to represent how hurt you think they are, 10 being
extremely hurt and 1 being not hurt at all.

## Rejection Sheet

| Name | Behaviour | Hurt Rating |
|------|-----------|-------------|
| Dave | | |
| Andy | | |
| Clare | | |
| Fiona | | |
| Friends | | |

5.  When everyone has completed their sheets,
    have the group report back.

## CONCLUSION

Consider the following questions in the whole
group:

• What would have been better action by the
  people in the story?
• Why is it that we often don't act as we
  should but act like the characters did?
• What can we do to help the relationships in
  our group so that these kinds of situations
  do not arise?

# Spiritual Climbs

## AIM

To think about our spiritual journeys.

## MAIN ACTIVITY

1. Pass out pens and paper to everyone. Put the instructions for constructing spiritual climbs, plus an example, onto the overhead projector or flipchart, or give everyone a photocopy. It can be a great encouragement to the group to draw your own climb as the example. If you are honest, this will encourage them to be honest too, and it will also make the exercise easier to understand.

2. When everyone has constructed their spiritual climb, divide into groups of four or five and ask each person to share from their chart.

### Instructions

Draw a cliff face which represents your spiritual journey. It may help you to think about:
1. Where was the going hard or smooth?
2. What were the overhangs you struggled with?
3. Where did you fall off and who pulled you back?
4. Who climbed with you at different stages?
5. What were the key moments in your climb; the pitons which secured your rope to the cliff face?

**3.** When everyone has shared their cliff faces with their group, brainstorm in small groups the things that caused people to fall off the cliff face, the overhangs that caused people to struggle and the pitons which secured their rope.

## SOUND BACK

Each small group reads its list, and a list for the whole group is compiled onto the overhead projector or flipchart. Talk about how the group as a whole can help people to grow spiritually. Discuss the following questions:

- How can we maximize the secure points in our group and in people's lives?
- Who has fallen off the cliff totally from this group and what can we do about it? How can we stop it from happening to others?

## GOING FURTHER

'The goal of our spiritual journey is to be more Christlike. We need to dig into our Bibles to find out how we can do this.'

## BIBLE INVESTIGATION

Ask everyone in the group to read:

- 2 Corinthians 3:18
- Philippians 3:12–17
- Philippians 2:1–8
- Colossians 1:10

Each of these verses teaches us important facts about spiritual growth.

- What are they?
- How do we apply these to our own group and personal lives?

# Just Good Friends

## AIM

To teach the group members to apply Christian values to their friendships.

## PREPARATION

Prepare six full-size paper human shapes. Label them 'Friend 1', 'Friend 2' and so on, and stick them up on the wall at the start of the session.

## WARM-UP

Play Hug Tag for about 10 minutes. In this game, one person is 'It'. He/she has to tag everyone. When a person is tagged they are out. If they are hugging someone they cannot be tagged. Hugs must be face-to-face, with arms round each other. No hug can last more than five seconds. You cannot hug the same person twice. The last person to be tagged is 'It' in the next game.

If some people never get hugged, and others get everyone wanting to hug them, don't worry, as this will help with the teaching session.

# MAIN ACTIVITY

1.  Give a copy of the friendship questionnaire to each person and ask them to fill it in.

2.  Collect in the sheets and ask people to share their answers to question 10 and any comments they might wish to make.

3.  Give an A4 sheet of paper to each person and ask them to tear it neatly into four pieces. Ask them to write on each piece one characteristic of a good friend. When they have done that they are to fold the pieces of paper up and put them in the bucket in the middle. Leaders also need to do this, but they should write characteristics that people don't often associate with best friends, e.g. smelly, spotty, lonely, bad at sport, unfashionable ... Think of ones appropriate to your group.

4.  When everyone has their papers in the bucket ask a volunteer to come out and choose six papers and to read them out and go and stick them on Friend 1. While he/she is sticking them on, ask for another volunteer to do the same to Friend 2. When all six Friends have their characteristics on them, ask the group to read them all.

5.  Ask everyone to stand by the Friend they would most like to be friends with. There should now be a group beside each Friend. The people in each group now share briefly why they chose that particular Friend. If possible put a leader with each group.

# BIBLE INVESTIGATION

The world often tells us what people should be like and who we should be friends with, but let's see what God's Word has to say about friendship.

*Group 1: Paul & Barnabas*. Read Acts 9:26–30; 11:22–26; 13:1–3.

*Group 2: David & Jonathan*. Read 1 Samuel 18:1–4; 19:1–7; 20:1–4.

*Group 3: Jesus & Peter*. Read John 21:15–19; Mark 14:27–31.

*Group 4: Ruth & Naomi*. Read Ruth 1:1–22.

*Group 5: Jacob & Rachel*. Read Genesis 29:10–30.

*Group 6: Paul & Onesimus*. Read all of Philemon!

# Friendship Questionnaire

1. Do you have any friends?....................................
   How many?....................Be honest..................

2. How many of your friends have larger feet than you
   and how many have smaller feet?
   Larger ......................... Smaller .....................

3. How many enemies do you have? ......................
   Are they larger than you?   Yes/No ....................

4. Write the name of your best friend backwards .....

5. Do you tell your best friend secrets that you don't
   tell anybody else? ...........................................
   List three..........................................Only joking!
   Why do you tell your best friends secrets?...........
   ...........................................................................

6. Has your best friend ever told other people your
   secrets? ..........................................................
   How did you feel? ............................................

7. Do you and your best friend ever:
   argue? ..............................................................
   fight? ...............................................................
   share milkshakes? ...........................................
   pray together? .................................................

8. If you didn't have any friends, what would you do at
   the weekends? ................................................

9. How many friends is it good to go around in a group
   with? ................................................................

10. How would you describe what a friend is? ...........
    ..........................................................................
    *This sheet will be collected in*

238

# (Action Adventure Walk)

## AIM

Outdoor team-building. A fun all-day activity suitable for a week or weekend away.

## EQUIPMENT

Maps, compasses and activity equipment.

## PREPARATION

An activity of this kind needs careful preparation and planning. The ingredients depend on where the adventure walk is to be held and the age and capability of the group. Draw up a treasure map based on the house you are staying in during your time away. The treasure is hidden on the site and is marked on the map. Construct the map so that it can be marked up and cut into jigsaw-type pieces in such a way that the treasure cannot be found until the puzzle is complete.

## ACTIVITY

1. Set the scene by giving the group the following information: 'You are about to be dropped in a foreign land in order to recover the long-lost and infamous "Lost and not found" treasure map. You are not the only group of treasure-seekers looking for the map; your rivals,

however, intend to use the treasure for wicked ends ... When in the foreign country you must not talk to any of the natives; they will recognize your accent and instantly betray you to the secret police. The roads are regularly patrolled and are best avoided.'

2. Divide the group into teams of five or six members.

3. Transport the groups by car or minibus and drop them off at a point unknown to them with the following: map, compass, walkman with no tape (optional – see below) and an envelope containing two 10p pieces. Leave them with the first clue:

'Your mission is top secret. To find your first target, ring [give telephone number].'

4. When they ring in, either have someone to receive the call or leave a message on an answer machine. The phone message is:

'The grid reference is: 40652971. 15 December 1984. Mrs Smith.'

5. At the grid reference given by the phone message is a graveyard and by Mrs Smith's grave is an envelope for each team with their next instructions in it. The envelope also contains a task for the group to do. If the task is completed the team receives as its reward a piece of the treasure map jigsaw and a surprise.

6. The grid references and clues continue, either as written instructions or even better, if you

have time, as tapes that each team listens to on their walkman and then leaves for the next group.

7.  As the groups move around the course, you will need to get a leader to each activity point just as the groups arrive there. This can be done with the same number of leaders as groups, providing the activity points are well spaced and the leaders use cars or bikes.

8.  When the groups have reached all the activity points, their last grid reference is for the base where they can put their maps together and find the treasure.

## EXAMPLES OF ACTIVITIES

1.  Find an item hidden nearby, e.g. a chocolate bar, can of food, fruit cake. (Food is always a good incentive and morale booster.)

2.  Retrieve cans of drink from a stream or pond using bamboo canes with string and a nappy pin or hook. Have the 'fishing rod' assembled or unassembled, depending on the age and ability of the group.

3.  Solve a puzzle, e.g. assemble a plastic shape into a cube. (There are dozens of commercial ones on the market which only cost about a pound.)

4.  Find lunch, using compass bearing and accurate measurement from an easy landmark. For example: 'In the bracken, 100 paces south of the trig point' or 'Buried in the sand 25 feet 170° from the No Bathing sign'.

Lunch should be in biscuit tins or plastic tubs and should have to be cooked, e.g. Pot Noodles, Vesta meals, tinned beans, soup, coffee, tea, hot chocolate. These can be heated either on a fire (check that it's safe and permitted) or on a camping stove.

**5.** *Break the code.* Devise a simple code and use it to write a message which each team has to solve (to their advantage!). The message could read, 'Don't forget to ask for the chocolate.' Using a simple alphabet code like this:

ABCDEFGHIJKLMNOPQRSTUVWXYZ
ZYXWVUTSRQPONMLKJIHGFEDCBA

the message reads:

WLM'G ULITVG GL ZHP ULI GSV XSLXLOZGV.

Use a level of difficulty in the code which reflects the group's ability.

**6.** *Disarm the missile:* You need the following equipment: bulb holder, baked bean or soup tin, 4.5v torch bulb in a bulb holder, 4.5v battery and three safety pins. The tin is the missile. To disarm it the group have to light the bulb for 10 seconds using only the equipment provided.

**7.** *Launch a rescue flare.* Equipment needed: lemonade bottle full of water, empty lemonade bottle, red paper streamer, reel of sticky tape, cork with a hole through it, bicycle pump and connector tube, bicycle valve, assorted bricks and stones. Their task is to launch the red streamer over 10 metres into the air.

# God's Smuggler

## AIM

A fun team-building exercise for an evening or weekend away. It involves dropping off groups of young people four or five miles away, and they then have to find their way back.

## EQUIPMENT

Map, compass, torch, instruction sheets.

## PREPARATION

Divide the group into teams of between four and six (depending on age and ability) and put a leader or junior leader in each group. (If you do not have many leaders, pull in a parent.) Decide if the exercise should be at night or during the day. Collect together the equipment for each group and choose the locations where you will drop the groups. Ask the group to assemble with appropriate footwear and clothing for walking. Brief your junior leaders on their role as foreign clergymen, emphasizing strongly that they are there to ensure the group's safety but not to intervene unless the group is in danger.

# ACTIVITY

Blindfold the group, lead them to a waiting minibus or cars and take them to your prearranged destination. When there, read them the following instructions, which you then leave with them.

---

## Instructions

**1.** You have been dumped at grid reference ..............

**2.** Your task is to smuggle a visiting clergyman to ........ without being arrested by the State Paramilitary forces.

**3.** You must observe the following:
(a) The clergyman is a foreigner unable to communicate with the group. (No speaking in tongues!)
(b) All 'A' and 'B' Class roads are patrolled by State Border Guards: you cannot walk along them, only across them.
(c) The Government has formed a number of groups to infiltrate and impersonate smugglers. Do not trust, contact or join any other group which you come across.
(d) All Public Houses have been notified by the Government of expected smuggling and therefore must be avoided at all costs!

---

# HINTS

**1.** Ensure that your leaders (who act as clergymen) keep quiet unless there is a real emergency, however lost, irate, frustrated and furious the young people get!

**2.** When everyone is back have a hot drink. Then debrief in one of these ways:

(a) Lead a group work exercise. Discuss: Who was the leader? Who was left out? How were the decisions made? Why did you go wrong?

(b) Use the activity as a discussion starter on the work of the International Bible Societies who translate and distribute Scriptures throughout hostile lands.

# Hot Pursuit

## AIM

A simple treasure hunt.

## EQUIPMENT

Balls of coloured wool, an envelope with instructions inside, a chocolate bar.

## PREPARATION

Cut coloured wool into 10cm lengths. On the day of the treasure hunt, lay out trails of wool. Tie pieces to plants, fences, gates, bushes, trees etc. Radiating from the starting point, the trails should lead off in different directions, the pieces of wool being a few metres apart. At the end of the longest trail place the envelope which contains instructions to find the chocolate bar. Place the chocolate bar in the correct position.

# ACTIVITY

**1.** Tell the young people that the object of the game is to follow the trail to find instructions leading to the treasure. The person who gathers the most pieces of wool will also win a prize. Explain that the trails lead in a number of different directions. The length of time the treasure hunt takes will depend on the length of the trails and how difficult the trails and instructions are.

**2.** When everyone is back, ask them to count their pieces of wool and give a prize to the person who collected the most (another chocolate bar!).

# Assassin!

## AIM

To get people mixing, to learn names and to break up cliques during a residential event.

## PREPARATION

Put the names of all the people present, apart from the Game Organizer, in a circle on a piece of paper. Keep the paper secret at all times.

Mary

Claire        Simon

John                Angela

Sue        Hilary

Peter

## HOW TO PLAY

1. The game is played throughout a weekend or week away, while the main programme is taking place.

2. Everyone is an assassin and the object is to be the last person left alive.

3. Each person comes to the leader to find out who his or her victim will be. For example, Mary has to kill Simon.

4. To kill their victim, they have to get them *alone*, put a hand on their shoulder and tell them that they are dead. A person cannot be killed if there is someone else in the room.

5. When people are killed they are not to tell anyone else that they are dead, nor can they tell the person who they have to kill who has killed them.

6. When Mary has killed Simon (refer to the diagram on the previous page), she goes to the Game Organizer and says that she has completed her assignment. Simon's name is then crossed out of the circle. Mary is now given her next victim's name, which is the next person alive on the circle.

7. Eventually, there are only two left and if they do not succeed in killing each other, the game is a draw.

## HINTS

1. The order of the names in the circle is important, as it encourages mixing between friendship groups and breaks up pairs or groups that are too cliquey.

2. Some rules need to be made on where people can be killed, e.g. boys cannot kill girls in the girls' shower room etc.

# Scavenger Hunt

## AIM

To get the group working cooperatively in teams to complete the greatest number of tasks in a given time.

## EQUIPMENT

Per team: a copy of the Task Sheet opposite (adapted if necessary to suit your group), a pencil, and if you decide to use the tasks as below, a wax crayon, a plastic rubbish sack, a sheet of paper and a plastic/paper cup.

# Scavenger Hunt Task Sheet

You have 60 minutes to complete as many tasks as possible. For each task where a signature is needed a space is provided. You may do the tasks in any order. NB there are different point scores for each task. The members of your group must stay together.

*Task 1:* Obtain a wax crayon rubbing of a police officer's cap-badge on the paper provided (25 points). Police officer's signature ......................................

*Task 2:* Visit the Chinese takeaway and obtain a menu signed by the person serving and all the customers (15 points).

*Task 3:* Obtain one of today's newspapers (10 points).

*Task 4:* Find a complete stranger who is willing to sign your feet and then sign here as well (20 points).
..................................................................................

*Task 5:* Go and sing a full Christmas carol at the Vicarage (15 points).
Vicar's signature ..................................................

*Task 6:* Find a stranger who will do a handstand for you, and get them to sign here (10 points).
..................................................................................

*Task 7:* Visit the Methodist Youth Group and offer to be their slaves for five minutes (15 points).
Methodist Youth Leader to sign here ........................

*Task 8:* Collect as many soft drink cans as you can find and bring them back with you (1 point for every different can).

*Task 9:* Find out what the ingredients of a Chicken Tikka are at the local Indian restaurant (15 points).
................................................................
Signed ................................................................

*Task 10:* Find someone who will sing the second verse of the National Anthem to you and get them to sign here (10 points).
................................................................

*Task 11:* Obtain the signature of the receptionist at the local hospital (10 points).
Signed ................................................................

*Task 12:* Obtain a cup of spring water (5 points).

*Task 13:* After 55 minutes return to the church hall and give the lady there a two-minute talk on what being a Christian means (15 points).
Total points here: ................................................................

# Crazy Car Rally

## AIM

A fun activity and integration event.

## EQUIPMENT

Maps and a set of clues.

## PREPARATION

Plan the car rally. Give the congregation notice in advance that the young people may ask them to drive for them.

## ACTIVITY

1.  Ask all the young people to get into teams of three.

2.  Announce that in two weeks we are having a car rally, the winner of which will win a mega prize!

3.  As none of your group members will be old enough to drive, they will have to find people willing to drive them around. Tell them that they cannot ask anyone from their own family or from the families of their fellow team members. They can only ask church members, but they can't ask any of the youth leaders.

**4.** Find out who is driving whom. If some of the young people are having problems finding a driver, have a few willing drivers whom the young people can contact.

**5.** The young people have to perform a series of tasks at different locations or solve a series of clues. The drivers are to follow the young people's instructions and are not to take the lead.

**6.** The drivers are not allowed to break the speed limit!

**7.** The winning team is the first one back with all the answers correct or the one to have completed the most when time is up.

**8.** Finish off with shared eats and drinks and give the prize to the winning team.

# Blind Numbers

## AIM

To develop teamwork skills and non-verbal communication.

## EQUIPMENT

One blindfold per person, and a large empty space or field.

## PREPARATION

Produce a copy of the Instruction Sheet for each team.

## ACTIVITY

1.  Disperse the team members around the field, making sure that they are well disorientated. Let them know their number, and tell them that they cannot do anything until you yell 'Go!'

2.  When all the teams are dispersed, yell 'Go!' Note the starting time and the time when each team finishes.

# Blind Numbers Instruction Sheet

**1.** Your task will be to line yourselves up in numerical order.

**2.** You must do this without any form of verbal communication.

**3.** Every member of the team will be blindfolded and dispersed around the field.

**4.** Only when the leader has led you away will you be given your number.

**5.** The numbers will range between one and the number in the team.

**6.** You will have five minutes of planning time before you are blindfolded and dispersed.

**7.** The team who do it in the shortest time are the winners.

**8.** When you think you have lined up in numerical order, call over the leader, who will say yes or no.

# Night Hike

## INTRODUCTION

Don't ask me why, but this is always a popular event – I suppose because it is a crazy idea which no one in their right mind who appreciates sleep would do. But it can be very worthwhile and successful if it is well thought out and well prepared.

## PREPARATION

You will need to consider the following points:

1. A letter to parents giving all the details of the event and obtaining their written permission.

2. Details to all the young people involved, with advice on clothing and what to bring, e.g. suitable footwear, waterproofs etc.

3. A night with a full moon!

4. A pre-planned course that can be safely covered in three to four hours.

Book a hall to camp in overnight which has facilities for cooking breakfast.

## PROGRAMME

A suggested activity programme for the event could be:

| | |
|---|---|
| 9.00 p.m. | Arrival at hall |
| 9.15–10.30 p.m. | Games |
| 10.30 p.m. – 2.00 a.m. | Walk |
| 2.00 a.m. | Return and sleep |
| 8.00 a.m. | Breakfast |

# Egg Race

## AIM

An outdoor, competitive challenge.

## EQUIPMENT

Eggs, paper and pens, timing clock with a second hand, Instruction Sheets and a minimum of two leaders.

## PREPARATION

1. Make copies of the Instruction Sheet and give one to each of the teams, a week before the race.

2. If you want to make it even more fun, why not challenge other youth groups in the area and send them an entry form, Instruction Sheets and a challenge poster? (Ask an artistic member of the group to produce one.)

3. Choose your checkpoint. It could be another church a couple of miles away, a hilltop, someone's garden (someone you know!). The important thing is the distance. It should be 1.5 or 2 miles away, and there must be plenty of different routes to get there.

# Egg Race Instruction Sheet

- A team consists of three young people.
- Each team must choose its own route and provide all its own equipment, including a means of cooking the eggs.
- The start and finish point is the church.
- When your team is about to start, you will be given three raw eggs to use in the race.
- Your task is to race to the checkpoint and cook and eat the eggs. (A leader will be at the checkpoint to ensure this is done satisfactorily.) Then race back to church.
- The winning team is the one whose aggregate time is the shortest (add together the times of all three individuals).

## ACTIVITY

1. Send one leader to the checkpoint and let all the teams know where it is, so that they can plan their route.

2. Start the teams at two-minute intervals and await the first arrivals back. As each person returns, write down their time and calculate team times.

3. The leader at the checkpoint must make sure that the eggs are properly cooked before being eaten. (N.B. Try to buy salmonella-free eggs!)

**4.** When everyone is back, announce the winners in reverse order and give a suitable prize, e.g. a cream egg each.

**5.** Close with an appropriate epilogue. You could talk on the new life which Jesus brings and 'eggsactly' how we can receive it! Don't crack too many egg jokes, or else they may become eggsasperated and the yolk will be on you.

**6.** Challenge everyone to a rematch next year.

# Prayer Paths

## AIM

To help the young people understand more about prayer.

## MAIN ACTIVITY

1. Person A talks to a partner (B) for one minute about what he/she has done over this last week, and the partner must listen without interrupting.

2. Swap over so that the listening partner (B) now has a chance to speak for one minute on what he/she has done in the last week, and Person A does the listening.

3. B now has to tell A all that A has done in the past week.

4. A has to tell B all that B has done in the past week.

5. Quickly debrief: Which was easier – talking or listening? Why was talking easier?

## TALK-TO

1. 'Today we are looking at prayer. Prayer involves not just talking to God, but also listening to him speaking to us. Before we look

at what we mean by talking and listening to God, let us try and identify *our own* understanding of prayer.'

**2.** Give out the Prayer Exploration Sheets for each person to fill in. Then briefly get people to share what they've put, e.g. hands up all who circled (a) for the first question.

**3.** 'Prayer is communication with God. How do we communicate with each other?'

Brainstorm for one minute – answers will include speaking, touching, writing, hearing, reading, actions, signs …

'Just as we have different ways of communicating with each other, there are different types of prayer. We are going to use the different types of prayer to build a Prayer Path.'

**4.** If you can get five paving slabs and label them P, A, T, H & S that would be great – if not, five large card squares similarly labelled would do. Lay out the squares one at a time in front of the group.

P is for Praise. We need to praise him for who he is, for his nature, for his majesty and spelndour etc.

A is for Admit. We need to Admit in our prayers that we have sinned and gone our own way, and repent and return to him.

T is for Thanks. Thank him for what he's done, in sending Jesus to die so you can be forgiven, for the new life of the resurrection, and also for the prayers he's answered.

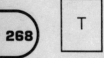

| H |

is for Hearing. Hear what he is saying, listen to the 'still small voice', meditate on scriptures he has brought to mind.

| S |

is for Something to ask for (the needs of others or yourself); or Speak your mind (tell God how you feel, be honest and open).

5.   Close with prayer, or go on to:

## GOING FURTHER

Divide the group into five smaller groups and give them one card per small group.

1.   *Praise*
Psalm 7:17
Psalm 60

2.   *Admit*
Luke 11:4
Psalm 51

3.   *Thanks*
Philippians 1:3–4
Philippians 4:6
Psalms

4.   *Hear*
1 John 5:14

5.   *Speak*
Psalm 99:6
Jeremiah 15:1
1 Samuel 7:8–9

Each group has 10 minutes to prepare a short prayer time based on their type of prayer, appropriate to the group. After 10 minutes bring the groups back together and let them lead through their prayers, then close with the Lord's Prayer.

# Prayer Exploration Sheet

*Circle your opinions.*

Prayer is:
- (a) talking to yourself.
- (b) only for old people.
- (c) communication with God.
- (d) a waste of time.
- (e) only done in church.

When we pray to God:
- (a) he ignores us completely.
- (b) we switch off our brains.
- (c) we build up a relationship.
- (d) we must have our eyes closed.
- (e) he will answer either Yes, No or Wait.

*Put an X on the line.*

I find prayer:
boring.........................................................exciting
easy.............................................................difficult
morning activity................................evening activity
easy with friends...............................easy by myself

*Rate 1–10 (1 = not important, 10 = very important for you).*

Daily prayer time      _____

Panic prayers      _____

Church prayer      _____

Youth group prayer      _____

# Affirmation Candles

## AIM

Group building and personal affirmation.

## EQUIPMENT

One candle per person, one large candle, one cross.

## PREPARATION

Create a mellow atmosphere – e.g. a quiet worship tape and subdued lighting. Arrange the seats in a semi-circle around the lighted candle and the cross.

## ACTIVITY

1. As people arrive, give them an unlit candle and ask them to sit quietly on a chair.

2. When everyone is gathered, turn the lights and the music off and let everyone enjoy the quiet.

3. Explain to the group that we are going to use this time to affirm one another. One person will go forward and light his/her candle from the one by the cross. Then, going to another person, he/she will say, 'I'm really glad you are a member of this group because ...' Then

they will light that person's candle with their own. They then blow out their own candle and return to their seat.

**4.** A third person can then go and light their candle from the one by the cross and do the same. The second person goes and says to someone why they appreciate them being in the group, and then lights their candle, and so on. If a person's candle has been lit by someone else, they do not blow it out after affirming someone.

**5.** The exercise will slowly build up, but try to stop the young people becoming slight in their comments. Make sure that everyone is included.

**6.** When everyone has a lighted candle, have a few moments of quiet and a prayer.

**7.** Blow out the candles and put on the low lights. Let people share what they felt and also any lessons they can draw out from it.

**8.** Finish with a quiet chat, or move on to something completely different.

# Prayer Photos

## PREPARATION

Before the group next meets, send two young people out into your town or village armed with an instant camera to photograph buildings, places and people that they feel it is important to pray for. They might want to photograph an old people's home, the police force, a local amusement arcade, a place where homeless people sleep: the choice is theirs.

## ACTIVITY

On the evening when your group meets, place the photographs round the room with a number next to each one. Give each member a pencil and paper on which to write what each of the places or buildings are or who the people are, and why they think it is important that they are prayed for.

# Video Psalm

Many of the Psalms give us verbal pictures reflecting the world and views of God.

In your group, create your own psalm to reflect your own culture, lifestyle and experiences. Use a video camera, words, music etc., *but* make it no longer than three minutes.

It could be a psalm of praise, thanksgiving, repentance, sorrow, creation, beauty etc. ... the possibilities are as endless as your imagination.

Read a few of David's Psalms if you are short on ideas.

# Circles of Prayer

## AIM

A check on how outward-looking you are in prayer.

## ACTIVITY

During a normal prayer slot in your evening programme, plot the focus of the prayers said on a diagram, without your group knowing. Draw a series of concentric circles. Label the inner ring 'Me', the next 'Family', the next 'Friends', the next 'My school' etc. to include the world. As people pray, plot the prayer with a cross. At the end show the plot to your group. Discuss the distribution of the crosses. What does this say about our field of concern in general and our concern for evangelism in particular?

# Prayer Calendar

Ask each of your group members to list anonymously their top three prayer concerns. Collate these and produce a prayer calendar for the month, with a different person, issue or thing to pray for each day. You will need perhaps to be flexible with some of the suggestions and make them appropriate for the group.

# More Than Words

Sometimes words are not enough – they don't express the pain and anger which we sometimes experience. The Bible tells us of people weeping, wailing, fasting, praying prostrate on the ground, tearing their clothes and screaming and shouting to God in prayer.

We need to encourage our young people to be honest and open in their prayers. Here are some thoughts on how to help young people to begin exploring this idea in their prayers and worship:

- Nail newspaper articles to a cross (you will need a large cross and nails): the act of nailing the articles to the cross is a way of 'giving up' situations into the hands of God and also provides a dramatic visual aid.
- Hold out situations to God while lying on the floor.
- Commit ourselves to:
  pray for the situation itself;
  act to change it;
  tell others of the situation.
- Declaration: we don't have to mumble our prayers, we can shout them to God as a declaration to him and to one another.

# Early Christians

1.  Prepare some of the young people in advance for this so that they each have a candle and a card detailing facts about an early Christian, which they will read out. The group sits in a circle around a central candle or focus. Quietly sing an appropriate worship song. Those with candles light them.

2.  The leader says: 'The Early Christians believed Jesus
    *   was worth suffering for;
    *   sets us free from sin;
    *   promises us eternal life;
    *   changes our life and our relationships.'

3.  The group members read from their cards and blow out their candles as they finish. (This needs to be done slowly and with dignity to be effective.)

## Paul

- Paul persecuted Christians until his conversion.
- He endured gruelling missions and founded many churches.
- He was beheaded for his faith in AD 64.

## James

- James was the younger brother of Jesus.
- He led the Early Church in Jerusalem.
- He died for his faith in AD 62.

## James

- James was the brother of John, a fisherman who followed Jesus.
- He was beheaded for his faith eleven years after the Resurrection.

## Peter

- Peter was the rock upon which Jesus said his Church would be built.
- He was crucified in Rome in AD 64.

## Bartholomew

- Bartholomew followed Jesus and was anointed by the Holy Spirit as a missionary.
- He was whipped to death in Armenia.

## Barnabas

- Barnabas was Paul's companion.
- He was the Son of Encouragement, used mightily by God.
- He was martyred at Salamis in AD 61.

# Candle Prayers

Candles have been used as symbols in worship since the earliest days of Christianity. Simple prayers around a candle can be a very effective way of encouraging your young people both to pray and also not to feel self-conscious about praying, as the room will be semi-dark!

1.  If your group has 25 members or fewer, sit around a single candle. If your group is larger than this, perhaps you will need to have more than one candle and to divide into groups.

2.  Ask the young people to sit and pass out pens and paper. Ask them to write down one area of darkness in the world and then place that piece of paper on the floor round the candle. Ask members to read out the pieces of paper, and then those who wish to can pray for some of the areas that have been named.

3.  End with the Lord's Prayer, or a chorus or song that everyone knows.